The House at
Ampasiet

Because we must never forget

For Victoria,

with much love

Love van Vuuren

Paula Kogel

Originally published in Dutch in 2005 as Ampasiet A 15
Translated by Rob Swain-Halberstadt
Editorial team: Peta Eisberg, Fran Howarth, Katherine Ross, Carolyn Fuller

This revised edition published in Great Britain in 2010

Matador
5 Weir Road
Kibworth Beauchamp
Leicester LE8 0LQ, UK
Tel: 0116 2792299
Email: books@troubador.co.uk
Web: www.troubador.co.uk/matador

ISBN 978 1848762 527

British Library Cataloguing in Publication Data.
A catalogue record for this book is available from the British Library.

Typeset in 11pt Sabon by Troubador Publishing Ltd, Leicester, UK
Printed in the UK by TJ International, Padstow, Cornwall

Matador is an imprint of Troubador Publishing Ltd

Paula Kogel
1911 - 2000

Contents

Foreword

"Heroes were always men; all the stories I'd heard said so. It was men who were brave, clever, wise, proud and saved everybody. Women were usually helpless and weak but good at having babies and bandaging wounds... Heroes protected women but didn't take them seriously... Women though, were not heroes."
(Ernest Hillen, The Way of a Boy, A Memoir of Java. P115)

It is now nearly 70 years since the creation of the Japanese prison camps of the Second World War in the Far East. Since then many words have been written about the terrible suffering of the interned male, military PoWs and no right thinking person would want to diminish these traumatic heroic stories. Nevertheless, I think it is equally important to remind ourselves that over 130,000 Western civilians were captured and interned in a variety of camps and locations by the Japanese in the Far East during that same period. Moreover, approximately 41,000 of these were women and 40,000 were children. Over 3,000 of these women were interned in camps in China, nearly 1,000 in Hong Kong, just over 1,000 in Singapore and over 2,000 in the Philippines. By far the largest group, however, were the 25,000 predominantly Dutch women and their 29,000 children who were captured and interned in camps in the former Dutch East Indies.

The women not only had to fight for their own and their children's survival, but many also endured the knowledge that their husbands or sons were interned by the Japanese. Some of these men were military prisoners of war who suffered extreme hardship and torture in such places as the Burma Death Railway or the Sumatra Railway. Others were civilian prisoners interned in harsh work and punishment camps where, towards the end of the war, even boys as young as ten to twelve years of age were sent. Many of those men, women and children who survived were scarred for life.

Paula Kogel was one of those women and *The House at Ampasiet* is her haunting story of how, newly married to a Dutch soldier, she followed him to the Far East to escape the war clouds amassing over Europe, only to end up, along with her two baby sons, in Camp Tjideng in Batavia (now Jakarta), capital of the then Dutch East Indies, now known as Indonesia. Camp Tjideng was one of the largest and harshest camps for women and children created by the Japanese during the war, reaching at its height more than 10,000 internees. Her husband was taken prisoner and transported to Burma where he worked on the infamous railway until its completion, and then transported to Japan for slave labour in a coal mine.

As Paula records, after the war the surviving civilian internees and the PoWs tried to rebuild their lives, mostly in silence and in the quiet acceptance that nobody was interested in, or fully understood their internment experiences. The fortunate families were re-united, others were torn apart by death or were eventually unable to re-adjust. Children who asked their parents about their experiences in order to understand the pain and suffering, were met with silence too. For the parents, the memories were too raw and the nightmares too real. The children who had survived the camps were left with deep scars and unresolved questions. Nevertheless, they too got on with their lives, but their questions and those of the next generation did not go away. Editing her mother's memoirs has, no doubt, answered many of those questions for Lore and her siblings and, perhaps, it will help answer some questions for ex-internee children and children of interned parents.

Undoubtedly, the intense poverty in Germany during and after the First World War, the enduring depression between the wars, and the traumatic experiences in Tjideng prison camp had a deep and lasting effect on Paula. As her memoir shows, her courage and determination cannot be over-stated; she displayed enormous amounts of both in surviving and caring for her two young sons throughout internment; she needed more to see her through the constant moves and separations from her husband during the post-war years and even more when she was forced to earn her living while raising her children after their divorce. There is no question in my mind that she, like so many other women who lived and raised their families through that tumultuous and traumatic period, is among the many unsung heroines of the Second World War and its aftermath.

Dr Bernice Archer

Note from the author's daughter

This book is a posthumous publication. Paula Kogel was my mother, born in Germany before the First World War, whose early life was marked by the ravages of that futile war and the abject poverty that followed after Germany surrendered. She made regular visits to Holland in the early thirties, where she met her future husband, my father. Anti-German sentiment was strong after the First World War, and the influence this had throughout her life is an important thread in her book.

Having survived the horrors of Camp Tjideng, she started writing her story in the mid-1960s, determined that this period in history should never be forgotten. Following her divorce she needed to earn a living for her family and had to put the book to one side to focus on building her career as a music teacher. When she eventually made a serious start on it again she was in her eighties and had to force herself to re-commit the now distant memories to paper. We would often find her slumped over her desk, weeping at the images of the harsh camp years that flooded back as she tackled the final chapters. Throughout the years she made persistent efforts to pursue potential publishers, without success. They commented that enough had been said about those years in the many books written shortly after the war ended, and people were no longer interested. She persevered but ultimately her health failed her and she passed away in 2000, without ever seeing her book in print.

I took on the challenge to have the book published in Dutch (in 2005) and now in English. Little did I know that I would embark on such a fantastic journey of discovery, finding fellow survivors who lived in the house with her, or who had lived in her house after the war. I have made some amazing new friends along the way, and it would have been wonderful if my mother had lived to see the book published and had been re-united with some of the people who had shared those horrendous years with her.

My mother's story ends when the camps are liberated, but many people who read the Dutch version asked what happened to my father during all that time, and how they were reunited and rebuilt their life after the war. In this English version I have therefore inserted a chapter recounting some of my father's experiences in the PoW camps along the Burma Railway and the coal mine in Japan, which are based on his own notes and family recollections, but written as part of my mother's story.

Part Three of the book is an additional chapter, written by me, based on my father's notes. It tells the story of my parents' reunion after liberation, with snapshots of what happened immediately after the war and their ongoing separations during the subsequent Indonesian war of independence, followed by the first few years of settling back in Holland, the 'mother country'.

For the Indonesian words and place names I have used the Bahasa Indonesia old spelling as was in use at the time, and for clarity have given the modern/English spelling of place names in brackets. Here and there I have inserted footnotes to clarify certain words or comments, or to refer to source material.

This expanded English version of my mother's life journey is dedicated to her determination and optimism to survive irrespective of any obstacle that was put in her way.

Lore van Vuuren-Ridings

Introduction

It was via the BBC WW II website that I first had contact with Lore, who had discovered my stories about my own mother's experiences in the Japanese internment camps. She sensed we had something in common and asked me to read her mother's book for some feedback. She was then busy preparing the publication of the Dutch version. I quickly got absorbed and for some reason I sight-translated it into English. This was not perfect by a long chalk and needed professional input.

In her story Paula does not dwell on the more gruesome and horrific aspects of her years in incarceration, although there are sufficient pointers, such as the utter cruelty of Sonei, the infamous camp commander, and his irrational punishment campaigns. Her story is more about how she and her sons, together with some like-minded friends, survived the hunger, despair and inhumanity by trying to stay dignified and human, sustained by her love of music. These years inside Tjideng were made extra difficult for her as she was a German woman amongst many Dutch.

A moving memorial service in Holland in 1965 sets the scene. Then, in Part One, we are transported back to 1942. Because of increasing fears about a Japanese invasion, Paula's husband Jan had been transferred from Surabaya to his new military unit in Batavia. The family embarks on a railway journey from the eastern side of the island of Java to the western side, taking more than nine hours and made at night for safety reasons.

During this journey many memories play out in Paula's mind. Presented as flashbacks, Paula reminisces about her life in

Germany during and after the First World War: growing up in post-war poverty, seeing pogroms and anticipating yet another war. But she also remembers the music and adventures she enjoyed as a kindergarten teacher, and cycling holidays in Holland - where she met her future husband, Jan. She thinks back to her civil wedding ceremony, which had to be 'by proxy' because, without Dutch citizenship, she would not be able to follow Jan to the East Indies.

In Part Two the family moves into a small two-bedroom house in a neighbourhood called Ampasiet, in the Tjideng suburb of Batavia. But, just as they are getting settled into their new house, the Japanese invade. Jan is taken prisoner and transported to the Burma Railway, while the Tjideng district is turned into a prison camp for women and children. Paula and her boys are imprisoned in their own home on street Ampasiet A. As the war progresses, thousands more women and children are herded into the camp to claim their 50cm of 'living space' allotted by the Japanese. Paula relates how her house gradually fills up, until she has to share her home with 21 women and children, suffering hunger, disease, physical and psychological torture, and total lack of privacy. And as life in the camp slowly disintegrates into an abyss of sorrow, she reminds us of the courage and determination of all the women to survive for the sake of their children.

It was a privilege to have been able to be of some little help towards realising the publication of both the Dutch and the English versions of the book. It is good that Paula's story is told. It is sad, however, that it had to take more than sixty years before this could be done and people were prepared to listen and read about it.

Roberte Swain-Halberstadt
Translator

Prologue

Holland, May 4, 1965

The pouring rain has drenched the earth. Bleached, anaemic earthworms wriggle in wide puddles that have formed on the roads and footpaths. Soaking flags hang half-mast above doors and windows, limp and lifeless. A church bell tolls once, very slowly, its echo choked in the damp air. The silent procession will soon get going: Holland is remembering its Second World War dead.[1] Slowly, the long queue of men, women and children, many carrying flowers, begins to move. I can see people cry. I am crying too.

Every year on May 4 I feel miserable. Memories overwhelm my mind and soul. I want to crawl into a corner and curl up, my face hidden, waiting for the day to pass. Tomorrow will be May 5, bringing with it just as many emotions as the day before. But away with all those awful thoughts and feelings! Come May 6, all will be different. Perhaps the sun will shine. There will be a future to look forward to once again.

And yet, I can't let go. The dreadful events of this century

1 Holland has two Second World War remembrance days. May 4 is 'Dodenherdenking' (Remembrance Day) when solemn ceremonies commemorate all the fallen, with air raid sirens marking the period of silence. May 5 is 'Bevrijdingsdag' (Liberation Day) and is a national holiday.

are so truly abhorrent and dehumanising that I cannot and do not want to forget them. How could God allow His and our paradise to become so besmirched, so dirtied, so terribly abused? All that wasted young life: whole families wiped out by ever more hellish, ever more refined weapons. Precious life, nature and art treasures – all burnt to a cinder. Why produce expensive bombs if you are never going to use them? What is the point of taking them back home again? For what? Just drop the lot! In the end, it is not our responsibility. Two men only were responsible: Hitler and Emperor Hirohito.

But, is that really true? I believe wars are caused by our own stupid, unthinking behaviour, our bad characteristics and lack of loving kindness. We all know ourselves with all our faults, but we don't accept the way we are and instead project our own malice on to others. How do we humans behave? Here is a simple example: Six-year-old Jantje is building a little boat, and it's looking beautiful; four-year-old Olafje is building a plane, and it's looking beautiful. They both finish and admire their achievements.

Then Jantje says: "My boat is much nicer."

Olafje promptly 'drops a bomb' on Jantje's boat. Jantje grabs Olafje by his blonde curls and shouts: "That's your fault, so now I'll smash everything that's yours!" The next day they start building boats and planes all over again and say: "These are much nicer."

Jantje and Olafje are my sons who were with me in a Japanese prison camp for women and children in the Dutch East Indies where, for three-and–a-half years, we had to fight for our survival. Because life is a precious gift.

The sun edges its way bashfully through clouds rimmed

with gold. It is May 4: Remembrance Day. Men, women and children lay flowers at the foot of monuments to commemorate their slain compatriots. Yet there is still no monument for the Dutch men, women and children who were incarcerated in the camps in the Dutch East Indies. We don't belong. For us, there are no flags at half-mast. We have been waiting for twenty years now for a gaily fluttering flag to celebrate our liberation, as well as *our* end of the Second World War, on August 15, 1945.[2] The sirens are wailing, as if to say: 'watch out, any day can be the start of a new war; each day could be the last.'

The sirens also wailed when, in February 1942, the war reached Java in the Dutch East Indies, or *'Insulinde'*[3], the Emerald Isles.

Coming back to my little Jantje and Olafje. They still had innocent little souls then. I fiercely believe in an honest and loving upbringing, and an unbiased teaching of history. Alas, there are no guarantees that such an education would bring the intended success. I hate war!

2 Since 1988 there is a monument in The Hague, known in The Netherlands as the 'Indiesch Monument' with an annual commemorative service in August.
3 A poetical name for the former Dutch East Indies, now called Indonesia.

5

PART ONE

Tempo Doeloe
The Good Old Days

Night Train Surabaya to Batavia – 1942

Surabaya, January 1942

A light dusk had settled over the city after a hot and balmy tropical day. The setting sun had turned the horizon aflame. Just half-an-hour longer and it would be dark, for in the tropics, day and night are divided equally into twelve hours of day and twelve hours of night. We were in Surabaya railway station, waiting on the platform for the night train that would take us to Batavia, where Jan had to join his new army unit. It would be a long journey, climbing high through mountains, plunging down into dark tropical forests, and winding through the villages and towns of Java. The train had been delayed. Jan inspected our luggage yet again and seemed satisfied for the moment. Our fellow passengers were talking in small groups. Such was the crowd that we were, whether we liked it or not, forced to eavesdrop on their conversations, which apparently were about the war in Europe and the expected Japanese invasion in the Dutch East Indies.

A woman asked: "Do you think there will be war here as well?"

"Oh no," a man said, "and if the *Jap* tried, he would be given a flea in his ear! Nah, he won't come here!"

"Now listen" said another, "they said something like that

at home too, but the *Moffen*[4] still trampled us underfoot within a few days."

"Yes, of course, that goes without saying. We weren't at all prepared and …"

"Holland is never prepared. They are always too late," another man interjected.

"You are absolutely right."

"Yeah, a Dutchman would rather sell you cheese to put on your bread, or biscuits to nibble with your tea, and go to church on a Sunday wearing a hat."

"Come on, friend, don't exaggerate. We had a good army."

"A token army, you mean?"

"Well", continued the man who had just been interrupted. "What can you do against such a superior power?"

The woman wanted to save the situation and said, "Oh well, let's hope the war in Holland will be short-lived. I am worried sick though, because if we were to believe all the news, the Jap is already well on his way."

"They can expect a warm welcome from our marines, with the most modern warships and fighter planes. The KNIL[5] has been well trained."

"Don't make me laugh!" someone said.

"Here comes the train," cried out the woman. "You might as well stop squabbling. We can't do anything but wait."

While they were making their way towards the railway carriages someone quickly added: "Don't worry too much. There are still the Americans, and they dearly love our oil in Borneo."

"Australia is much closer," said another. "Oh, I don't want to think about all this. First let's find a good seat."

It was nearly dark when the train rolled into the station, to

4 Moffen is the Dutch derogatory name for the Germans.
5 The Dutch East-Indian Army.

the sound of a piercing whistle and spewing smoke, finally coming to a screeching halt. There it stood, like a gleaming, long, thin iron snake, menacingly black and surrounded by greyish-white clouds of smoke that blanketed the platform in a humid cloud. The lights of the locomotive and a few lanterns barely lit the now dark station, and in the sparse beams of light everything took on a ghostly hue.

Jan first put the luggage in the corridor and then took hold of little Jantje[6] to lift him onto the train. The child started to scream.

"Mummy, Jantje not go in black snake." He wrenched himself loose and wrapped himself in the pleats of my skirt.

Jan became cross, grabbed the child and pinned him against the suitcases. I hastily clambered onto the train, to comfort Jantje, carrying little Olafje in my arms. We looked for our compartment and, while singing a lullaby, I quickly made up a bed for the children and then gave them something to drink. Luckily they soon fell asleep. Little Jantje still sobbed every now and then and murmured something in his dreams. There was a smile on his dear, fat little baby face. Thank goodness, he'd already forgotten the parts of the journey that had frightened him.

"Jan, couldn't you have been a bit more patient and gentle with us?" I asked.

"Sorry Paula. You know how nervous I always am when we travel. I can't help it."

"Oh well. We are safe in our seats now", I replied.

6 The suffix 'tje' in Dutch denotes something small. In the case of family names, the Dutch often name children after their parents (usually fathers) and then add a 'tje' to indicate they are the juniors.

A few minutes later, the train made a bumpy, jerky start. We were leaving Surabaya, the beautiful city of flowers; the city of international attraction; the city that I would never see again.

On the rhythm of the train

Peace and quiet! Time to relax … *boo boom, boo boom, chu chu, boo boom, boo boom, chu, chu* …relax to the rhythm of the train.

Jan had nodded off and the children were breathing evenly in their sleep. I opened the curtains and gazed at the full moon.
"Hello my friend, I love you," I whispered.
"Will you keep me company tonight? I can't sleep. I want to dream, enchanted by your silvery light."
I surrendered to musings about the course of my life. Images from my youth in Germany were floating past as brief flashes.[7]

I am sitting with other children on the edge of the pavement. It is a pleasant summer evening and a cool breeze is rippling through my hair. Suddenly, men with their hands raised stiffly in the air in front of them walk by, calling "*Sieg, Sieg.*" I was three years old and it was August 1914. The First World War had just begun.

Standing at the top of a stairway leading down to a coal cellar, making the children sing a song, I think that I have mastered the art of conducting. After trying just a bit too hard,

7 Paula is going back in time regularly during this railway journey. To denote such flashbacks, this shape ⁖ has been used to mark the beginning and end of such reminiscences.

I fall down the stairs, resulting in a swollen and sore nose. Even as a five-year-old you can literally, and figuratively, fall flat on your face.

Hetti, my school friend, has died. All the children may come and say their goodbyes. She lies there so radiant in her coffin: she almost looks like a bride. At the cemetery, the school choir sings. Now Hetti is with the angels. Big, brown leaves cover the other graves. My mother says: "Every day a long train arrives, filled with wounded soldiers."

The fourth winter of the war, in 1917, is very cold. On both sides of the streets the snow piles up on the pavements, swept up by shivering old men and women. Along icy, slippery roads small emaciated horses pull carts with provisions to their distribution points. The big and strong horses have all been requisitioned by the army. The civilians are now beginning to experience shortages because the army has to be fed properly. Despite a beautiful sunrise, the mood of the population is depressed. We kids, however, are enjoying the winter. Warmly wrapped in shawls and hats we slither to school. The small icy tracks on the paths become more and more slippery and turn into a shimmering steel-blue colour. In the school playground stands a life-sized snowman with shiny eyes made of coals, a fat orange carrot as a nose and a pipe in his mouth. December, the best month of the year, is already a week old and each child is in thrall of Christmas, the finest festivity. Nativity plays are being rehearsed and the schools resound with happy children's voices singing the age-old Christmas carols.

On the kitchen table lays a mountain of knitwear: socks, ear warmers, woolly hats and big scarves, warm gloves, as well as all sorts of provisions. My mother and sisters are busy packing everything carefully in a cardboard box, to be collected the following day by a white lorry with a large, red cross painted on it.

"Mummy, who will get that parcel?"

"All soldiers at the front will get one at Christmas because they are not living in a house, but in the trenches."

The Red Cross lorry has departed, and my half-sisters Ellie and Erna sing a sad song about a soldier who is sure he will be killed and will never come home again.

'*Christmette*' – Midnight Mass: the service will start at six o'clock in the morning. For the first time in my life I am allowed to go to that celebration. It is still pitch black. Stars twinkle and the frozen snow crackles under our shoes. When the big bells start to toll I squeeze my mother's hand. I do not know what is happening to me. The deep, melodious sounds take hold of me: I am at one with their rhythm and resonance. I want to stand still and fold my hands in prayer. But we quicken our pace and through the wide open church doors we see the bright shining lights of the tall Christmas tree. In the church, my father has to find a place on the benches on the right-hand side. In those days, men and women still had to sit separately from each other. I find it strange that I am not allowed to sit between my mother and father, but that's how it used to be. In the aisle my mother says: "Now you have to walk tiptoe and not say a word, because here *wohnt der liebe Gott*." (God lives here.)

To the right of the altar stands a very large Christmas tree in full splendour, bedecked with real candles, soaring up almost into the arched roof of the church. The verger had lit the last candles with a long stick. The resonance of the bells dies away in the lofty space, just as the organ starts up with loud chords. I am startled and huddle close to my mother. I had never heard anything so awe-inspiring. That music could be so wonderful! The organ pauses for a moment and then a sea of voices breaks into exultant song. It is like the power of a breaking wave; and I sing along. The minister ascends the pulpit, greets the community and tells us about the child in the manger.

While he is talking about the soldiers at the front, I slowly begin to understand the connection with what is happening in the world, as seen through the eyes of a six–year-old. If I felt any pity inside my heart, I did not know it then.

Maybe only now I understood with a sudden shock the newspaper article my father had read to me, which as a three-year-old I had been too small to comprehend:

"December 28, 1914,
News from the Western front: as everyone knows, because of Christmas, an armistice has been announced by the army leaders of the three countries at war. From noon December 24 till midnight December 27, the cannons will be silenced. Thanks to the efforts of the Red Cross, all soldiers and officers will have received a well-filled Christmas parcel in the week before Christmas. The German population has shown its compassion for their husbands and sons who storm the barricades to offer themselves up for 'People and Fatherland.' Early this morning on Christmas Day our boys emerged from the terrible trenches and, sitting on the ramparts between cannons and trees and ruined houses, enjoyed the sunrise. A young singer loudly started the Christmas carol known throughout

*the Christian world. The soldiers sang 'Silent Night,
Holy night' and the 'enemy!' sang along in their own
language. A moment of peace?"*

My mother comes home with her meagre shopping.
"I have just seen it again" she says.
"Long trains filled with wounded soldiers are going past.
They are not stopping."

The train to Batavia was slowing down. Looking out of the
window I saw the contours of a small town. To be fair, 'town'
was rather a grand word for it, for there were no street lamps to
be seen, let alone streets. In the moonlight the place seemed
deserted. I thought it might be one large *kampong* (village), or
several smaller ones all joined together. I saw black roofs
amongst the coconut trees with, here and there, some white
washing hanging limply on a line.

Tradesmen never sleep if there is money to be made. They
were there before the train had even pulled into the station.
They had put their yokes with baskets on the ground, and
displayed the contents on *tikars* (bamboo matting). In the
sparse light of wicks burning in small tins filled with oil, we
were tempted by *loempiahs* (spring rolls), rice wrapped in
banana leaves, *pisang goreng* (fried banana rolled in pancakes),
sweet cakes, *spekkoek* (a kind of layered cake) and coffee
tubruk (a kind of Turkish coffee). Who would not like these?
For beer lovers, there were tins of beer chilled in a box filled
with ice.

As Jan got off the train to buy us a snack, a guard walked
alongside the train on the platform to check if the curtains of all

the windows were drawn. After a little while Jan returned and, dishing out our 'supper', said: "The train has to take on water and that will take half an hour. Let's eat now, before all the shuddering starts again."

"Just let me take care of the children first, Jan."

The boys had woken up by now and when Jantje realised he was in the black snake after all, he started to cry again. I sang our lullaby once more and gave him a biscuit and something to drink. Then Jan gave Olafje his bottle, and peace and happiness reigned in our little family.

The train slowly started to move as the traders contentedly packed up to leave.

"*Tabeh tuan, tabeh nyonya* (goodbye Sir, goodbye Madam), have a good journey," they called. They saluted, for they knew that most of the travellers were soldiers of the Dutch East Indian Army (KNIL). The KNIL soldiers, in their fetching uniforms with blue capes and high caps, were highly regarded in Holland. In 1936 they formed the guard of honour at the engagement of Princess Juliana and Prince Bernhard.

In the meantime I had switched off the light inside the compartment and opened the curtains.

"I will snuggle up in my corner again, if you don't mind. Aren't you going to sleep, Paula?"

"I can't sleep with the full moon, you know that."

Jan started humming a song that we often sang together. He had a beautiful voice.

Guter Mond du gehst so stille,
In den Abendwolken hin,
Bist so ruhig, und ich fühle,
Dass ich ohne Ruhe bin[8]

Who doesn't feel romantic and sensitive by the light of the moon, that supreme celestial body? The atmosphere had me in thrall once more. The train fell back into its rhythm again… *boo boom, boo boom, chu chu, boo boom, boo boom, chu, chu …*

My thoughts take me back once more to my home in Germany in the years following the First World War. I see the past as clearly as if I was watching my life in a film, the images as vivid as if it were yesterday. I hear my mother say: "If you do not stop reading immediately, I will box your ears. Here is a billion-mark note. Hurry down to the grocer's and ask for a pound of sugar. Run, will you, otherwise the sugar will be gone and the money is worth hardly anything as it is."

After the First World War the French had occupied the Ruhr area and had totally ransacked it. Everyone was unemployed and had to survive on just a small government handout, except the black marketeers, who we called the '*Neureicher*' (newly rich). Inflation was a horrendous spectre: a billion marks for a pound of sugar.

The war and the revolution were in the past, but our unwelcome guest '*Hunger*' refused to leave. Emperor Wilhelm had fled to Holland some time ago. He would very probably not starve over there.

There is one incident that preys on my mind because I feel awful about the way that I behaved. At secondary school we learnt French and sang French songs. I loved the language. Once,

8 'Good moon, you move so quietly, through the evening clouds, you are so restful and I feel, I have no rest at all'. From the fourth couplet of *Guter Mond*, a well known German folksong partly written by Karl Enslin.

a French soldier stopped me in the street, smiling broadly, and offered me a large piece of chocolate. I only knew such delicacies from advertisements. Oh, how I would love it.

But what did I do? I hid my hands behind my back and said: "*Merci monsieur, mais je n'ai pas faim.*" (Thank you sir, but I am not hungry.)

How could I have been so patriotic? He surely knew how difficult it was for the German children. Afterwards, I felt sorry for the soldier. He had wanted to do something good and was rejected.

During the years after the First World War, we discussed that war at school and in youth groups. We could not figure it out, just did not understand how it was possible that something so dreadful could have happened. Communism was on the march. We just did not know anything anymore, us young people. And then someone came into power who was also opposed to the communists. Moreover, he sorted out the country's finances. My mother was able to buy real coffee and bake cakes again, and there were jobs because the coal mines were re-opened. In short, that man who had been born in Austria at the Czech border gave the people '*Brot und Spiele*' (bread and fun), had '*Autobahnen*' (motorways) built and gave every worker the right to own a '*Volkswagen*' (peoples' car).

But my brother, a fervent Social Democrat, said: "*Pass auf, der Hitler macht Krieg.*" (Hitler will wage war). Many said the same, but their warnings went unheeded. Other countries knew it too, but did nothing. Lord, forgive us for being unable to resist material wealth; we who kept our ears and eyes closed. But we had been so terribly poor for such a terribly long time.

The train stopped abruptly and remained motionless in the middle of nowhere, its lights extinguished. What on earth was that? Jan looked out of the window and said: "I hear aeroplanes. The Jap is probably scouting around for the best spot to land."

We heard people talking excitedly. A guard walked past without a lantern and commanded: "Stay inside! There is nothing going on."

We, and I think everyone else on the train, could feel the threat of dark clouds hovering over our heads. A few minutes later, the train got going again and continued its usual rhythm, while the moon reappeared in all her clarity from behind a mass of white clouds. It was getting cool, as we were approaching the mountains of Middle Java. I covered the children with an extra blanket and put on my cardigan. The cool air was a relief after the oppressive heat of the past hours.

"Another hour and we will arrive in Yogyakarta where we can go outside during a longer stop. Aren't you bored, darling? Staying awake all night is not for me. What were you thinking about the whole night?"

"*Tempo Doeloe* – the good old times, Jan. It is very interesting. *Tempo Doeloe* is a magic lantern, or a *laterna magica*, if you like. The images appear chronologically, as in a film, and in the magic light of the moon it is as if they are projected onto the dark jungle or a similar landscape."

"Do I also play a part in these images?"

"Oh yes," I said with a laugh. I went to sit next to him and snuggled up in his arms. Together we stared at the moon and Jan asked: "Shall we sing '*Guter Mond*'?"

"We'd better not, the children may wake up and I also find

the song a little melancholy. Do you know that Jantje's eyes often fill with tears when I sing a lullaby at night?"

"Maybe he has an ear for music. And our Olafje?"

"Our second one only thinks of eating and sleeping for the moment. We do have lovely children, don't we, Jan?"

But Jan was no longer listening. Once again, I was alone with my thoughts.

Mother's Day in Holland – 1965

The Padre

One day in 1964 I received an unexpected visit. The task in hand, that had been demanding all my concentration, would just have to wait. But I hoped that in a little while I would be able to force my mind back again to those awful conditions that, long ago, held my life, together with that of so many thousands of women and children, firmly clenched in an iron grip, the experiences of which would be forever etched in our minds. After many years of making notes and writing down memories, I had finally started writing, in German, my mother tongue, about the desperate fight for survival in Tjideng, the infamous Japanese camp for women and children in Batavia in the Dutch East Indies, where from February 1942 until August 1945 we had been interned by the Japanese invaders.

My visitor introduced himself: "I am Padre Hamel. I am a minister who has worked and suffered together with Dutch, British, American and Australian prisoners of war during the Japanese occupation of the Far East. Much more than their physical suffering, it was the psychological torment and mental anguish endured during the building of the Death Railways in Burma and Thailand that led to such a total mental disintegration, the likes of which I have never experienced during normal times."

Padre Hamel was of medium build with grey, thinning hair. He had an air of warmth and great culture, with a loving interest in people. He radiated a tranquil benevolence.

"I know all about it, Padre, because my husband survived those horrors and told me a little bit about it, although not very much. What he did tell me was that a Japanese soldier saved his life by pushing a chicken egg underneath the bamboo matting every day, despite running the risk of his own execution."

The Padre continued: "That is quite possible, Madam. But thousands of men became total wrecks or did not survive. Fortunately, I was able, together with a Catholic colleague, to help the wounded spiritually and give the dead Christian burials. Believe me, the graves are countless. Luckily, after the war ended these graves were well tended to, with the help of the local population. Now every grave bears a white cross with a name and a date."

"But now, the reason for my visit. You were probably trying to guess. Many men who did not survive entrusted me with messages in the hope that their families would one day get to know what had happened to their loved ones. Your good friend Jo told me many things about himself. He gave me your name and a photograph of himself, together with a few meagre personal belongings, in the hope that you might still be in touch with his parents. That is the reason for my visit. Jo had a very difficult time but, after many good conversations, died peacefully in my arms."

"I think I know how to contact Jo's parents, Padre. Leave it with me. I still keep in touch with Christel and she knows where his family lives."

When I told Padre Hamel that I had started writing a book about our experiences in camp Tjideng he showed great interest and then added: "I would like to tell you that I too have written a book about those years of horror and humiliation. It is called '*Soldatendominee*'. Alas, only a few copies were sold because nobody in Holland was the least bit interested at the time.[9] It has caused me a lot of sorrow that the Dutch population was so hard and unfeeling towards their compatriots from the Dutch East Indies. All those repatriated ex-prisoners of war who returned 'home' had no place or future in Holland and were left to their own devices to just get on with it. God grant them peace."

He stood up, ready to go. "Please don't go yet, Padre. I still have so many questions."

"Please, ask away."

"Will humans always bring such suffering upon themselves? Will there never be an end to war? It seems to me that it is always the mothers and children who are the ones who are really punished for the sins of men."

He replied with a loaded question: "I take it you know the Bible well?" I nodded affirmatively. "Well, in that case you will also know that the inner struggle of the human soul started with the fall of a beautiful and disobedient angel, Lucifer. He wanted to be better than God Himself. Do you recognise that wish?"

"Certainly, this can be found in all the fairy tales and myths of nearly all civilisations. But can't God in His Omnipotence intervene?"

"No. God has given us our own free will and that is the law

9 'Soldatendominee' [Padre] by J C Hamel, published in 1948 by W van Hoeve Publishers in The Hague, and dedicated to "All the parents whose sons never returned".

of nature, which cannot be avoided. *With one's own free will to do the right thing under whatever circumstance.* And another thing: God doesn't do mass manipulation. He works with everyone individually. From the way I have heard you speak this past hour, you have already experienced this yourself. Am I correct?"

I couldn't do anything but nod in agreement.

"We have it within us, all of us, believe me. Within each atom of our being resides a small, but ample part of God's Spirit."

"Padre Hamel, I feel such pity for people and animals that are drawn into all those wars being waged now anywhere in this world or those that will inevitably happen in the future."

"My dear lady, may I ask you something? I can see that you love everything that lives, but that one person who did you harm, close to you or far away, do you love that person still?"

I did not answer immediately. Padre Hamel looked me in the eyes and said in a friendly voice: "*That* is the essential part of our existence: humanity and forgiveness; being able to love your enemy and to forgive him."

"I know, Padre: Matthew 5, verse 44: *But I say unto you, Love your enemies, bless them that curse you, do good to them that hate you and pray for them which despitefully use you and persecute you.*"

"But isn't that too difficult for us human beings?"

"If we never want to have a war again, then we must take these words to heart. But now I have to go; there is still so much work to be done. Keep on writing and when you have finished, translate what you have written into Dutch."

"Thank you so much for your visit and our conversation, Padre Hamel."

"It's been a pleasure. And, one more thing, Madam. I would

like you to have on loan this copy of my book *Soldatendominee*. Goodbye, stay healthy and keep on reflecting and, especially, praying."

He shook my hand firmly and, without looking back, walked towards his car.

Not long after I had returned the book to Reverend Hamel, I received a parcel, containing the book and a note from him, saying he wanted me to keep it after all, in memory of our dear friend Jo who passed away in Burma.

Mother's Day

Jan and I separated in February 1965. 'Divorce' is such a terrible word, a word full of hurt. First of all I will need to rediscover myself and figure out how to move on from here. Jan and Olaf, my two sons who had endured the horrors of the camp with me, both became sailors and had already left home. My daughters Lore and Liesel were born in the Dutch East Indies after the war. To be alone with two teenage girls is not going to be easy and I will need to think of something to supplement our meagre budget.

Pondering all this, I sit gazing at the May sun, low in the sky and bathing the trees, plants and flowers in our front garden in a soft pink haze, slowly bringing the day to a radiant close. Outside on the pavement children are talking, singing and now and then playfully jostling one another. Across the square a few doors open; worried mothers think their darlings have been playing long enough now and are calling them inside for the evening meal.

Evening peace is all around us, in this peace-loving country, a balm for the soul. Lore is reading by the light of the lamp and Liesel is busy with the record player. "Mum, just listen to this record, will you. It is the latest of the Beatles. You'll love it."

"Yes, that song '*Yesterday*' is very beautiful."

In 1956 all former inmates of the war camps in the Dutch East Indies had suddenly received a payment of 275 guilders (then approx. £150); compensation for three and a half years of deprivation. I can't remember who had been so generous: Japan or our own government. We bought a record player with the money.

Lore looks up from her book and says: "Mum, tomorrow we will get up early and you must promise to stay in bed, for we want to surprise you."

"Wonderful, who wouldn't want to be surprised for a change? You are making me very curious."

The girls received a dress allowance and could decide for themselves how to spend it. Lore always knew what she wanted, loved organising things and could manage her pocket money. Sometimes scouring the shops for just the right dresses took a little too long for my liking. Then I would say: "I will wait just half hour longer. If you haven't found anything suitable by then, we will go home." Lore would always find something quickly, but Liesel could never decide and did not want to be helped by her mother or her sister. So she would end up in floods of tears instead of going home with a nice dress. But we just went back home without. It probably sounds harsh, but the result was that both girls developed good personal taste. Those independent decisions taught them to dare to make demands themselves. The girls are also rather proud of their exotic birthplace and consider themselves little globetrotters.

"Everything in this house is just so old-fashioned."

"Yes," says Liesel, supporting her sister's opinion, "everything should be changed."

"Dear girls, it is a lovely evening for a story. Shall I tell you how we left the Dutch East Indies in 1950 and arrived in this country?"

"How was that journey?" Liesel asks. "What kind of boat was it?"

"A thirty-year-old British coal cargo ship without railings, the *MS Amarapoora*, with an Indian crew. After the war it was used as a troop ship to transport ex-KNIL soldiers back to Holland, but this time the cargo consisted mainly of women and children. We had to sleep in the hold on the floor or in hammocks. That was our home for three weeks. And we were reminded daily that this was most certainly not a luxury passenger liner. This tired old coal ship struggled slowly through the waves and when we wanted to be on deck we would get bits of soot from the chimney in our eyes."

"Mum, it almost sounds like a slave ship."

"One day we were on deck reading, knitting or talking. Suddenly someone said in a whisper: 'Shhh, don't be afraid, but look.'

"Lore, you stood there watching the waves, right by the edge of the ship where there were no railings. I forced myself not to panic, thinking 'what should I do?'

It was dead quiet and everybody was looking at me: what will the mother do? I called out very softly: 'Lore, come and have a look at what Mummy has here.' The tension was unbearable. Then you turned round and walked straight into my outstretched arms. You were just under two years old and already very independent.

Of course, I could no longer let you walk freely around the

deck without putting you on a leash, but you would not have accepted that for one moment, so you had to go to the children's crèche."

"How old was I then?" asks Liesel. "Did I do anything that I shouldn't have done?"

"You were a seven-month-old baby lying ill with malaria in the ship's sick bay. There were Dutch nurses on board who assisted the English doctor in emergencies. One morning something happened that frightened the life out of me."

"How exciting, Mum. What happened?"

"A nurse came to me and said, 'I arrived just in time with the morning bottle for your baby.'

'What was the matter?' I asked her, getting worried.

'Your baby had pulled herself upright using the silver bell that is hanging from a red cord attached to the mosquito net and somehow managed to get the cord caught around her little neck. Fortunately everything turned out okay. But I can't think what might have happened if I hadn't removed the cord immediately.' She handed me the little bell. 'Thank you, thank you so very much,' I said, and embraced her spontaneously."

"I'm lucky I'm still here," says Liesel, "but *that* was some journey!"

"That was not all. We only saw your brothers during meal times and in the evenings, and I was never very comfortable with that. There was an MP (Military Policeman) on board who was keeping an eye on all the youngsters, especially the boys. On the lower deck at the bow of the ship was an open porthole through which the boys would stick their heads to watch the fish.

The MP told me: 'I am here virtually all day to keep an eye

on them, for you never know what may happen if they push each other. I scared them off by telling them that, if someone should fall overboard, they would be eaten immediately by the sharks. But that lad over there, standing as punishment in the corner beneath the stairs, would not be frightened. He wanted to see the sharks for himself.'

That was Olafje. 'Listen to that gentleman,' I admonished Olafje severely.

'Yes, Mum.' he replied. I made Olafje stay by my side for the rest of that day.

Jantje came running towards me and said in English, in one breath 'Good morning Madam, good morning Sir, how are you?' Jantje had visited the Indian cook in the galley and had enjoyed a good meal, he told me. But that visit had an unexpected sting in the tail. The captain stopped me as I was leaving and requested politely that I should not allow the children to fraternise with the Indian workers, because that was not how Europeans should behave. After the captain had departed someone said: 'Hmmm… how very colonial.'

But, now it is time for bed."

The following morning I keep my promise, and comply with my daughters' urgent request. At exactly nine in the morning the bedroom door opens, very slowly. The first visitor, squeezing himself past Lore's legs, is our Paljas. He was a mixture of dachshund or tekkel and pinscher, and we sometimes called him Pikkel. Some people thought he was a new breed.

Lore manoeuvres the large tray past the bedroom door and places it on the bed. Paljas had already jumped onto the bed but has to be shooed off immediately. Our beautiful brown pointer,

Slamper, enters the room together with Liesel. Licking my hand softly, he shows that he has a better pedigree than the mongrel. Liesel spreads a plaid blanket over the end of the bed for the dogs. They both leap on it immediately amid much growling and gnashing of teeth. My daughters are sitting on either side of me and the bed is positively crowded. Four pairs of eyes look at me intently so I open my first gift. My daughters' taste delights me. That little ceramic vase, decorated with brown raffia and bought at '*Het Oude Ambacht*' (The Old Crafts Shop) is still my most precious memento of that first Mother's Day without Jan.

The excellent breakfast is highly appreciated by everyone. As soon as Paljas figures out that the tray is now devoid of any tasty bits, he creeps under the blanket. Slamper scratches around on his part of the blanket as if trying to make a nest, turns round and round and finally collapses with a deep sigh. A little later we hear him snore. How delightful, the simple things in life.

Liesel leaves the room and returns with a school atlas.

"Mum, our geography lesson was about Egypt and the Suez Canal. Didn't our boat sail through there?"

"Absolutely," Lore comments, "otherwise we would have had to sail around the Cape and that would have been a long way round."

I am tired of my overcrowded bed and promise my daughters that I will continue my story about the boat journey after the evening meal of *nasi* (a fried rice dish), by candlelight, and accompanied by the music of an Arabian lute.

Suez Canal

Dusk slowly descends on the square where we live. Only in the month of May can the green of trees and bushes be that delightful, bright luminous colour. Nature is quiet, as if saddened by the end of a beautiful day. Lore lights a few candles and Liesel puts on a record of lute music. Slamper and Paljas are sleeping peacefully on their mats. The atmosphere is quiet and warm.

Liesel asks: "I have a question, Mum. Is this lute music different from the music you play?"

"Oh yes, this music is played on a traditional Arabian lute. The original name of this very old instrument is 'Oud' or also 'Ud', and the Arabic 'al-ʿûd' became *lute* in English, *luit* in Dutch and *Laute* in German. The oldest lute and the music you are hearing now were found in the tomb of Senmut, who was the private tutor of the Egyptian princess Neferura, daughter of Egyptian female Pharaoh Hatshepsut. The most treasured musical instruments in ancient Egypt were the lute, harp, dulcimer and flute. The sound of a lute is love. Let's listen a while and then turn it down a little as background music to our story."

"We boarded our coal ship in 1950 and, towards the evening of a very hot day, the ship glided slowly into the Suez Canal, leaving behind the 'Bittermeren', a series of small lakes at the mouth of the Canal. The setting sun turned the desert on either side of the canal into a flaming glow of orange and purple. The slow-moving ship cut a triangle of foaming white waves in the water. Opposite, in what remained of the red evening sky, a pale disc of the moon could already be seen rising in the East. As the light dimmed, the moon started to brighten to its full glory, shining like silver. If you closed your eyes slightly, it felt as if you could reach out and touch the beams of light. Despite the ventilation fans, droning continuously, the heat in the hold was still suffocating.

When everyone was asleep, I crept quietly up the stairs to the upper deck and settled myself in a deckchair. The bridge was lit up and every now and then a member of the crew would walk by. A little distance away from me I heard two people whisper. It was as if the silence wrapped itself as a cool sheet around me. Far away I saw the dark contours of a mountain range, possibly the Sinai, and at the other side was Egypt, a civilisation that was more than 3,000 years old. Biblical stories passed through my mind, while everything I had learned and read took shape, whether they fitted together or not, because everything was so overwhelmingly multifaceted. Then from the desert came the clear tone of a shepherd's flute, sounding as pastoral as the lute music on the record.

I stayed there dreaming for a while longer before going back down into the hold to make sure that everything was in order with you kids and to catch a few more hours sleep myself. The monotonous grinding of the engines and the sound of water lapping against the ship's hull lulled me to sleep. When I awoke it was daylight and they were saying that in an hour we would be in Port Said.

Port Said was a noisy and busy city. Every Arab had something to sell and tried to attract the attention of the arriving and departing passengers. They even sold little chicks and showed their knowledge of Dutch by calling '*kippetje hier, kippetje daar*' (little chicken here, little chicken there). Boys dived into the water to retrieve coins thrown overboard by the

Europeans. Back on the quay side, sitting in a circle, they counted their spoils. From Port Said we sailed into the Mediterranean, on our way to Holland, where we would have to build a new life. So we go where we 'belong', to Europe. The Dutch East Indies no longer exist. It is now called *Indonesia Raya*. But we will never forget our old 'Indië'. It will be kept alive in our thoughts and in our world of memories."

"And now, goodnight, my dear youngsters, sleep well."

"Goodnight, Mum, and thanks. Until tomorrow."

Peace descends. The dogs yawn noisily: they are asking for a quick sniff in the garden and then to bed. When I open the door to the garden, the candles start to flicker. They were only little stumps now producing long trails of smoke. It's not a very pleasant smell, but I like it. In the clear, starry and moonless night I hear the sound of a goods train die away, its rhythm slow and monotonous. I must have something with trains, I thought. Tomorrow I will write again about the night in the train from Surabaya to Batavia, accompanied by the fascinating full moon.

How did I actually get to Holland and the Dutch East Indies; I, who loved her own country and language so much?

Paula with her classmates from the Teacher Training College, 1932. The lute clearly was a very popular instrument.

Paula (left, with lute) and her pupils for a performance of Rumpelstiltzkin – Immendingen, 1936.

Paula brought much joy and laughter.

Paula as kindergarten teacher in Pommern.

Paula (left) with her sister Johanna in Amsterdam – around 1933.

The 'Pied Piper of Hamlin' on the 'bolderwagen' in Pommern.

Paula met Jan in 1932 during one of her cycling
holidays in Amsterdam.

Jan in the KNIL uniform – Nijmegen, Holland, 1936.

Jan's sisters Bep and Co.

Jo, close friend of Jan and
Paula, who died on the
Burma Railway, as told to
Paula by the Padre when he
came to visit.

Berlin 1938 – its famous avenue *Unter den Linden*, looking out towards the Brandenburg Gate.

The *MS Christiaan Huygens*.

The wedding in Balikpapan –
12 January 1939.

Dreaming on the beach at Balikpapan on the island of Borneo – 1939.

Tempo Doeloe: Jan and Paula with friends in the 'good old times' before the war.

Farewell to Europe

Holidays in Holland

As a teenager in Germany, I spent my school holidays each year in Amsterdam, with my sister Johanna. After the First World War, having received news that her husband had been killed at the Eastern Front, she moved to Holland with her little boy Bernhard. Determined, and with a good head for business, she had worked hard in Amsterdam and built up a profitable ice cream parlour. She married a Dutchman who was a mixture of a Communist and an adventurer. He indoctrinated Bernhard so much that, against Johanna's wishes, they both left for Spain in 1936 to fight in the Civil War on the Communists' side. They did not survive this adventure so Johanna had to continue life alone and support herself.

Sometimes I would make the annual trip to Amsterdam on my bike, via Oberhausen and Arnhem, and would then stay in a small hotel in Arnhem. On one of those stays I got covered in fleabites, but happily forgot all about them the following day as I cycled along a beautiful cycling path through woods and heath between Arnhem and Ede. I suddenly had to stop for a flock of bleating sheep crossing the road, and a girl cycled to a halt alongside me and started a conversation. I got the gist of what she said, although I did not understand all the words. We switched to that universal language everyone understands: music. Cycling along, we sang Dutch and German songs, also a gorgeous tear-jerker popular at that time, and had great fun. We did not know anything about each other, not even each other's names. It did not matter, because it was one of those casual meetings we would remember all our lives. Near Wolfheze she turned left and called "*Tot ziens!*" (See you) and a few times "*daag, daag, goede reis!*" (bye, good bye, have a good trip). I called "*Auf Wiedersehn.*" But we both knew that this would never happen. Singing, I cycled on and finally arrived very saddle-sore in Amsterdam. My sister was glad to see me and laughed. "Yes, I am sure you are saddle-sore, it's your own fault. You could have travelled much more comfortably by train."

After a day's rest I could enjoy lively Amsterdam again. On one of my walks in Amsterdam's city centre park *Het Vondelpark* together with 'Spits', Johanna's dog, I was amazed to see love-struck couples demonstrating their feelings with loud kisses while riding their bikes.

In the mornings, when the windows were opened, you could be sure to hear the bread delivery boys with their handcarts, loudly praising their delicious wares, while singing popular Italian arias, because singing really was their forte. That always made my day. On top of all that, the *Theater Carré*, one of Amsterdam's most famous theatres, was within walking distance from Johanna's home.

Every other day I would visit one of the beautiful seaside towns, not far from Amsterdam, to go sunbathing, because returning to school with a bronze tan would always guarantee everyone's admiration. The best part of the holiday was at the end when Queen Wilhelmina celebrated her birthday on August 31. In the evening there was a grand firework display on a large sandy field outside the city. Whole families went out there to enjoy the colourful display. "Ah's" and "oh's" resounded through the summer air. The highlight of the evening was also the finale: a large-as-life likeness of the Queen projected against the evening sky in wonderful colours, followed by our national anthem the *Wilhelmus*. Sadly there was not much spontaneous singing. I would have liked to sing along, for I knew the words in German. Ah well, that's how the Dutch are. That's when I learned a Dutch saying, which they sometimes also said to me: '*Doe maar gewoon, dan doe je al gek genoeg.*' This was one of those well known Dutch cynical sayings, meaning: '*Don't be so daft, your normal behaviour is mad enough.*'

There was, of course, another reason for my regular cycling holidays to Amsterdam. In 1932 on one of my earliest visits, I had met a handsome Dutchman called Jan, and we spent that vacation boating along the canals and exploring the seaside and nearby dunes. They were wonderful times. Of course, living in different countries, so far away from each other meant we did not see each other all that often, although Jan did once cycle to Germany to see me. Mostly, we had to make do with letters.

But these were unsettling times because, just like everywhere else in Europe, Holland suffered a deep depression after the worldwide economic crash of 1929, and this caused widespread poverty. To help subsidise the meagre family income, Jan had been forced to find work and abandon any plans for further education. Unemployment was rising fast, but the state unemployment benefit was miserly, causing a lot of unrest among the population. When the government announced a further reduction in benefits in 1934, protests broke out in cities across the country, including Amsterdam. In one of its oldest neighbourhoods, the *Jordaan*, some particularly violent riots took place where the civil and military police meted out fairly harsh treatment to the protestors.

In order to ease the unemployment situation, the government decided in 1935 to set up subsidised work camps as job creation schemes for the unemployed, who were set to work mainly on large-scale public works. The well-known Amsterdamse Bos, a lovely park to the south of Amsterdam, is the result of such a project. These camps proved to be extremely attractive as they provided food and medical assistance. It was not long after that Jan also lost his job and he decided to apply for a place in one of the camps for the young unemployed rather than hang around at home, begging his mother for pocket money, or suffer his father's truncheon practice. Jan's father, a strict man, worked for the Amsterdam Police, at one of the most notorious stations in the city, and was involved daily in skirmishes with unemployed protestors. Rather sadly, he was known to use the truncheon at home for the occasional punishment.

Unfortunately, by 1936, unemployment had risen to such an extent that the authorities were fast running out of funds and had to ration these work camp opportunities. From then on people were only allocated a single period of eight weeks and, as Jan had already been there for three periods, he had to leave. One of the women who worked in the kitchens in his camp had lived on the island of Java in the Dutch East Indies for a long time, and she gave Jan the idea of joining the Royal Dutch East Indies Army (KNIL). Jan joined up, thinking that escaping Europe and all its misery might be the best course of action. We decided to get engaged before he left and I would follow him to the Far East as soon as my work in Germany would allow. What we did not realise was how quickly Jan would be called up for duty after successfully completing the very heavy initial training programme.

On December 31, 1936 he set sail for Borneo in the Dutch East Indies on board the MS 'Indrapoora'.

Pommern

A high ranking civil servant in an immaculate brown Nazi uniform called on me and asked in a harsh voice: "Why do you want to leave our beautiful country?"

I refused to be intimidated and answered just as curtly: "I explained the reason in my letter of resignation. As far as I am concerned, it is a good enough reason."

He changed his demeanour and said with a smile: "Would you not like to consider your decision a while longer? You are a very good employee of ours."

He paused for a minute and made an even bigger effort to appear charming. Everyone knew him as a self-complacent and vain man. Leaning towards me he said: "We had already decided to offer you a very high position."

"My decision is made," I answered brusquely.

"Do you know what that will mean for you?" he asked. "You will spend your whole life feeling homesick for your country and language."

"So be it," I said, "for freedom of spirit comes at a price."

He greeted me with 'Heil Hitler' and disappeared stiffly.

After this official interlude, everything just happened in a whirlwind. I booked a train to Berlin and from there to Amsterdam, so keeping my promise to my Dutch fiancé Jan. During the journey to Berlin I thought with sadness in my heart about my life back in Pommern, now called Pomorska and part of Poland, even though every kilometre was taking me closer to Jan, across the oceans and through foreign countries.

I had held a fascinating position as a child development teacher in Pommern where, as part of a compulsory education project, primary schools were being set up in various farming villages. It was not easy, because the farmers refused to cooperate and kept their children at home. I had to think of something original to make the school seem attractive to them and came up with a great musical idea. The farmer who had put me up had a '*bolderwagen*' (a four-wheeled open farmer's cart). I put the youngest child in it, and got two older children, together with a dog, to pull the cart along. I played the recorder, just like the 'Pied Piper of Hamlin'. All the other children followed as we made our way through the village, and the mothers joined eventually. That's how I won the confidence of the children's parents. The end of the procession was always Camin, at the edge of a lake. The Caminer Bodden are lakes named after the old German town Kammin, now called Kamien Pomorska, in the Northeast of Poland.

I knew that I would never again see this country called Pommern and during the journey drank in the beauty of this landscape, a fertile region, the granary for the surrounding countries. In summer the nearly ripened grain would wave to and fro in the balmy, salty wind of the Baltic. Long white beaches adorned the coast line, and inland there were woods and delightfully blue lakes, which I called 'God's eyes'. Along the coast were Hanseatic towns with warehouses and dwellings built in the Dutch style.

As the train slowly approached Berlin station, I placed my luggage in the corridor. It was not much, because I was only allowed to take two suitcases and some hand luggage. The amount of cash that could be taken out of Germany was also restricted. One of the cases contained some very personal possessions from which I just could not bear to be parted: my Lutheran bible, the Edda, Homer, Goethe, Schiller and other German books, song books and, of course, my lute. All these would make life for me and my fellow sufferers a little more bearable in those dreadful circumstances looming ominously on the as yet distant horizon.

The afternoon sun cast its oblique rays over Berlin: evening was approaching. Riding in a taxi along 'Unter den Linden', Berlin's magnificent boulevard, a long, straight thoroughfare that runs through the centre of Berlin in full view of the Brandenburger Gate, I saw that the Nazis were not only clearly present, but had everything '*gut im Griff*' (well under control). Columns adorned with eagles and swastikas lined both sides of the road. Sometimes the taxi had to stop for a marching group of singing 'brown-shirts'.

When I arrived at my hotel a porter immediately rushed towards me to take my luggage. At the reception I booked a room for one night. I tried to shake off the fatigue of my journey by taking a cold shower and putting on some fresh clothes. Afterwards, I went downstairs and was looking forward to a cool glass of wine. It struck me that in the lounge and nearby function rooms virtually all the tables, apart from a few occupied by families, had been claimed by soldiers in uniform. People were talking in hushed voices. At one table close to the reception desk was a group of young lads, at the most about twenty years old. One boy apparently thought things were too quiet. He got up, raised his glass and started to sing. One of his comrades grabbed him by the shoulders and pushed him back into his seat. The atmosphere was oppressive.

I was sitting at a table opposite an older soldier. After excusing my intrusion, I asked, "Sir, could you please tell me what's happening here?"

He was silent for moment, looked at me seriously and said: "Madam, at exactly midnight our trains will depart for Czechoslovakia. No guesses what that means."

I suddenly felt an ice-cold shiver running down my spine, and my heart started to beat fast. It was the autumn of 1938. On the wall behind the reception desk a radio started to crackle loudly. The low humming of voices stopped immediately, and a loud, cold and clipped man's voice announced: "The planned action has been delayed; all units return to barracks."

It remained quiet for a few more seconds, as if the meaning of the announcement had not yet sunk in. But then a cheer went up and soldiers threw their caps into the air. Everyone stood toasting one another with filled glasses. The waiters could not bring wine and beer fast enough. As if on command everyone started singing. It filled me with joy to listen to so many young voices. What were they singing?. No, not 'Deutschland über alles', but a lively soldier's song 'Auf der Heide blüht ein kleines Blümelein, und das heisst: Erika.'[10]

---

10 'On the heathlands a small flower blossoms, and it is called Erika.' From the first couplet of a German folksong by Herms Niel.

Someone called loudly "And now toast for peace. All count to three, 'bottoms up', empty your glass in one swallow and throw it over your shoulder; you are not allowed to look back." I took part together with my unexpected table companion. Believe me, it was an unforgettable moment. It temporarily made us forget the threatening clouds of war.

Goodbye to my room

Amsterdam Central Station was, for the time being, the end of my journey that had started in Pommern. It was October 1938 and I had just seven weeks in which to get legally married and obtain Dutch citizenship, while my future husband was far away at the other end of the world. Because I could join Jan in the Dutch East Indies only as a legally married spouse, this meant I had to 'marry with the glove' or 'marry by proxy'; originally the man standing in for the bridegroom would be wearing gloves, in order not to touch the bride. There would be no actual gloves involved, but in my case a handsome young man. This was Maarten, Jan's younger brother, who would take Jan's place at the town hall and would be guarantor for the legality of the marriage. It was all very fascinating, but I had to admit that I started feeling a little panicky because I did not know Jan's family at all. During my short vacations in Amsterdam I had never visited them.

There I stood, all alone on the platform, clutching a letter from Maarten and his photograph. Uncertainty suddenly overwhelmed me to such an extent that I was considering jumping on the train waiting at the other side of the platform that was ready to depart into an easterly direction.

'The darkest hour is just before the dawn.' My dawn salvation came in the shape of my sister Johanna, who could speak Dutch because she had been living in Amsterdam for some years. She would sort things out for me. I was convinced of that. I walked straight into her arms. How wonderful it was to have a sister like her, with her twinkling eyes and lovely smile.

Hanging above the front door of my future in-laws' house was a sign proclaiming '*Welcome amongst us.*' Johanna had visited the family beforehand, so the introductions were made spontaneously and without any shyness. We all had tea and biscuits and Johanna made sure the conversation went smoothly. Still, I did not feel entirely at ease, because 'Pa', as he wanted to be called, observed me constantly with his penetrating, dark eyes as if waiting to trip me up for some misdemeanour. Later, when I remembered that he was a policeman, it all fell into place. 'Moe' turned out to be a lovely woman with a keen sense of humour. She said she could also speak a little German and put her money where her mouth was by saying, "*Heute Kartoffeln mit Zwiebeln.*" (Today's dish is potatoes and onions). Everyone laughed and there was a good atmosphere. Bep and Co were lovely sisters-in-law and just as curious as any other teenagers; they had many questions that I was not yet able to answer due to the language barrier. Only Maarten could speak fluent German. However, one day he said: "My dear sister-in-law, nobody here speaks German…"

He laughed and did not finish his sentence.

I added: "And after speaking Dutch all day, I go to bed every night with my head buzzing".

After the ceremony at the town hall on November 21, 1938 we had a party, joined also by Jan's friends. I had met most of them before on my cycling holidays. I discovered that my father-in-law was a lot more fun than I had initially thought. One time he took me to a football match at the stadium, taking it for granted that I would love it. Afterwards we went to an Amsterdam *brown café* for a beer. Only once, when I mentioned that I wanted to say one last farewell to my family, did he start to speak about the situation in my homeland.

"Pa, I don't want to talk about it. Please let me be happy. I am really looking forward to life in the Dutch East Indies. But I must go home to say goodbye to my parents before I set sail."

My parents lived in Westphalia, not far from the Dutch border. The whole family, or at least those who lived in the area, were present. A delicious smell of '*Kaffee und Pflaumkuchen*' (coffee and plum cake) hung in the air. Everyone had their own opinion regarding my departure for distant shores. Some thought it would be a fantastic adventure, whilst others had many objections to my going.

My mother said sadly, "I know that I shall never see you again, my dear child, but I hope everything will turn out well for you."

My half-sister Ellie handed me my lute and we all sang, just like in the old days. '*Am Brunnen vor dem Tore da steht ein Lindenbaum*' from *Die Winterreise* by Schubert. My brothers had already said their goodbyes.

"I think a drink will do me good," my father mumbled.

My mother and I were alone.

"Mum, sometimes I feel such doubt, for some Dutch people look at me strangely, as if they are reproaching me for something. Mum, do you think there will be a war?"

She did not reply.

"I would like to tell you something I've never told anyone. I was doing some shopping in the town where I worked, it must have been in 1934 or 1935, and a police band was marching through the streets playing some joyful marching music. Children were following the band, just like they always do all over the world. Out of the blue, I suddenly had a vision. To my right I could no longer see houses, but instead there were enormous red, orange and bright blue flames. The musicians marched straight into the flames, continuing to play happily as they went. I was so overwhelmed that I had to turn away in order to avoid people seeing me cry. I have never been able to forget that vision. I would often see those images clearly before my eyes. And lately I can't seem to shake it off. Mum, I am so scared."

"I know, my dear child, we are all afraid. Try and forget it. Once you are together with your husband everything will be fine."

At that moment we saw people running around, shouting: "They are at it again."

"What's going on, Mum? What's happening?"

In the centre of the town we saw what the Nazis were up to. In the middle of the market square was a fountain with a statue of a horse and rider, the town's symbol. Once, after our school exams, we had placed a bonnet on the rider's head because we wanted to protest against the, in our view, negative and narrow-minded thinking of the town's council. Around the market square stood beautiful white houses, three or four storeys tall, as well as elegant fashion stores and all sorts of other shops. Whole families were being taken from the houses, the people roughly manhandled and pushed into lorries. Their furniture, books and even grand pianos were being thrown out of the windows. As usual, it was the Jewish people who were being targeted. The old Russian word *'pogrom'* had also found some willing ears in my country. My Jewish friends lived in the suburb. What would happen to them? Little Ruth, who had come to me for lute lessons, and Frank, a medical student and a talented photographer? I was often a guest of the family. I felt powerless, furious. Words could not describe my indignation.

"Mum, what kind of inhuman people are these?"

My mother answered sadly, "They are in power now, my dear. They rule the roost. We are too late and we cannot turn back the clock."

My dear mother took me into her arms because, whether I wanted to or not, I had to cry. "I think I am glad I'm leaving, Mum. This is no longer the Fatherland that I know."

When I returned to my room, which was still the same as I had left it before my departure for Pommern, thoughts and memories raced through my mind. This was the place of my youth. Through a wide window I looked down onto the flower garden below, which I had always looked after. My father did not think much of it because flowers were useless and wasn't a vegetable garden just as beautiful? I did understand my Dad. A farmer can't deny his origins. After bad harvests and deaths in his family he had emigrated to Westphalia from East Prussia. He often told stories from Mazuria, a land full of dark woods and blue lakes. He taught us ballads and we would sometimes sit there shivering with fear as he told us tales about ghosts, spirits, devils and witches. Although the stories disturbed our sleep, we still kept on asking for more.

East Prussia now belongs to Poland and Russia. Köningsberg, with its famous university, is now called Kaliningrad, capital of Kaliningrad Oblast, the Russian enclave between Lithuania and Poland on the Baltic Sea. The statue of

Kant, the great German philosopher, still stands there. The university, now called The Immanuel Kant State University of Russia, attracts many students from across Europe, and it is very moving and touching that many of them feel compelled to look after and restore the dilapidated war graves from the First World War.

But it was time to say goodbye forever to this little space of my own. I had to let go of the memories of dreams during balmy summer nights, lit up by a full moon, with the air intoxicated by the fragrant privet that grew beneath my bedroom window. Goodbye to this place of my first love, to feelings of loyalty and friendship, and to any fantasies about the future. But remnants of my dreams and desires will live on within these four walls after I have left. Goodbye room, goodbye house, farewell.

Insulinde

On the *Christiaan Huygens* to the Dutch East Indies

Back in Amsterdam, after my final family visit to Germany, my parents-in-law must have noticed how quiet and downhearted I had become. I think that they understood the reason for this, for they neither alluded to it nor enquired about it. To cheer me up, Moe invited me for a lovely day out shopping in town for the journey, followed by a cup of tea in the *Bijenkorf*, Amsterdam's large department store. She bought me a large cut glass vase and said, "You'll be needing that in the Indies because there are always flowers in bloom there." It made me laugh because Moe had hit exactly the right note with her uncomplicated, practical Dutch nature. Then it was time to say our goodbyes: Pa and Moe, my sisters-in-law Bep and Co, Maarten and his fiancée Rie, and my dear sister Johanna. I owed all these people so very much; how could I ever repay them?

"No problem," they said. "Just write."

Moe whispered in my ears: "Grandchildren!"

There she was, the passenger ship *MS Christiaan Huygens*, a floating castle, moored in Amsterdam harbour, ready to depart. The ship made an enormous impression on me. For centuries the Dutch have been used to the sea. But I, a real landlubber, was more at home wandering through woods and fields from one youth hostel to the next with little money to spare, carrying my rucksack and lute, forever singing and on the lookout for like-minded souls. I stood there, looking up in awe at this ocean steamer, which would be my home at sea for the next three weeks. What an experience it would be, visiting distant countries together with new friends, for I was sure that I would be meeting many interesting people on the journey. I felt as if I had hit the jackpot. And at the end of the long journey Jan would be there, waiting for me, at the quay in Balikpapan in Borneo.

The gangway was raised and the ship began to move. I was too excited to feel the pain of saying goodbye. Suddenly there was a sea of white, waving handkerchiefs; my sisters-in-law had brought a big towel, which of course was visible for far longer than any of the handkerchiefs. The ship slowly gathered speed as she glided serenely through the Amsterdam-Rijn canal in the direction of the North Sea. It was December 1938, two weeks before Christmas. Two years previously, on December 31, 1936, Jan had made the same journey to the distant Dutch East Indies aboard the *MS Indrapoora*.

I was lying on my bed in the two-berth cabin, feeling deeply miserable and as sick as a dog. Was this the dreaded seasickness? I wished I were dead. What had I done to deserve this?

When the ship had sailed into the North Sea, where a heavy storm was raging, people had begun to leave the deck as it started to rain. The waves were growing higher, taking on the colour of dirty green glass, and were battering the hull. I loved it and, thinking of Jan, started to sing a song by Schubert:

'Dem Schnee, den Regen,
dem Wind entgegen,
im Dampf der Klüfte
durch Nebeldüfte,
immerzu ohne Rast und Ruh.'[11]

Someone tapped his finger against his head as if he thought I was mad, and disappeared. I was the last to stay on deck, until the smell of the engine oil penetrated my nose. That's why I was now lying on my bed, cursing my fate.

I shared my cabin with a friendly, dark-haired girl. Her name was Esther and she was on her way to the Dutch East Indies together with her parents. On Christmas Eve, '*Heiligen Abend*' in Germany, I sat by myself in the cabin and felt homesick for the first time. Home was so far away. Why had I ever left my country? I took my lute and started to sing my favourite Christmas carols, when Esther came in, listened for a short while and then shut the door again.

After dinner, Esther's mother introduced herself to me and said: "Dear madam, please do not think my daughter was impolite when she heard you sing. It wasn't that at all. She came to me crying and said she felt homesick when she heard you sing those beautiful Christmas carols."

I said I was sorry, for what else could I say. I was invited to come and have a glass of wine with the family. And that's when I heard the sad story of just one of the Jewish families.

"We are Jews and have been living in Holland for several

---

11 'Through snow and rain and wind, in the spray of a gorge, through mist, always restless and without peace.' Schubert: Rastlose Liebe ("Dem Schnee, dem Regen"), song for voice & piano, D. 138 (Op. 5/1)

years," Esther's father began. "But Berlin was our beloved city where we and our grandparents were born, and where we were so very happy. I was a teacher of German literature. Believe me, we were German, totally rooted in the German culture. Three men in our family fought for their country in the First World War and never returned. But now things are happening that make life there unsafe for us, and we have lost confidence. We decided to emigrate. And as you can see it is going to be the Dutch East Indies."

I discovered there were more Jews on board, seeking a new life away from Europe. We often stood at the railing discussing all things under the sun, with the moon big and full in the sky and the shiny, moon-drenched waves lapping lovingly against the ship's hull. The atmosphere was restful and filled with peace.

Mrs Goudsmit, a somewhat elderly lady, had taken it upon herself to chaperone the young married women travelling without husbands. She kept us, five girls and also two young male teachers, together. She had lovely stories about her previous voyages and would relate funny anecdotes from the *Jordaan* in Amsterdam. She had most likely done this journey before, because she knew every harbour town and their tourist attractions. Our dear Mrs Goudsmit made a very good guide. She also prevented us from spending our money needlessly. We sometimes joked: 'Mother would prefer to hand us over personally, and without any harm, to our husbands.'

The *Christiaan Huygens* increased her speed, gliding graciously through the long swell of the jade-green Indian Ocean and, with streamlined perfection, sailed on to her destination.

Sometimes we were accompanied by a school of dolphins. I imagined they were laughing at us, inviting us with their loud splashing to a swimming contest.

Greek mythology tells the story of Dionysius, god of seas, sailors, drink and merriment, walking along the beach dressed in beautiful clothes and with a wreath of vine leaves around his head. The sailors on board a pirate ship moored in the harbour thought this was a lovely girl waiting for them, and decided to have a party. Dionysius let himself be abducted but once on board he made sure the sailors became very drunk and then he killed them and threw them one by one into the sea. Since then they say that dolphins are the souls of drowned seamen.

Luckily we are allowed to believe what we like but, in 1948, returning to the Dutch East Indies from leave in Holland, my firstborn son Jantje, who was to become a sailor, stood at the railing of the *MS Oranje*, staring into the Red Sea and called out: "Mum, come and have a look. I can see them, the Egyptians with their horses and chariots." He was seven years old. That's how thoughts and images rise up from our memory, multi-faceted and ordered, turning our thinking into a captivating game.

Boo boom, boo boom, chu chu, boo boom, boo boom, chu, chu …
I suddenly noticed that it was almost pitch-black, and realised I had been daydreaming for a very long time on the train to Batavia.

"What's the matter, Jan? It is completely dark."

"Nothing special, darling, we are only passing through a few tunnels and then the train will stop in Yogyakarta."

"It's rather damp and there is a musty smell, don't you think?"

"The tunnels are only short. It won't take long before we are through and then we'll get off in the beautiful city of the Sultan. I am looking forward to it."

"How long will it be before we arrive in Batavia?"

"We are already more than half way into our journey. I estimate another three or four hours."

With squeaking brakes the train rolled into the covered station of the medium sized town Yogyakarta and, blowing off steam just once or twice, halted at the platform. Here too the lighting was sparse. Waiters offered cups of steaming coffee and snacks.

"Jan, you go outside. I'd rather stay here with the children. Should you come across some nice Yogya silver, would you please mind getting me some?"

The city was known for its very artful and beautifully crafted silver objects. The basic inspiration for each piece of art, whether they were jewels or utensils, was the mythical bird 'Garuda'. No European would leave the Archipelago without having bought some of this art. So this is where the Sultan lived. What would this Javanese head of state think about a Japanese invasion of his beautiful country? I would never know.

Jan returned from reconnoitering the city and said: "A walk at night through this place isn't as nice as I had thought. Only a few shops were open and of course there were the street vendors."

He handed me a small package saying: "You'll surely like these."

"Thank you very much. I will admire them in a minute."

The children had woken up and the train was about to depart. I opened the little parcel to find a little pendant on a silver chain, a ring and some earrings, all in Garuda style. They were beautiful. The lovely pieces of jewellery survived the war and became hotly contested heirlooms.

I became curious once more about my nightly companion, the moon. First, I switched off the light and then opened the curtains. There was my friend, but in a different position. I fell back into musing and was once again on board the *Christiaan Huygens*.

The ship had completed more than half the journey, the final destination being Surabaya. Impatience and expectation hung like a haze over our heads. Couldn't the ship sail faster? Is she tired perhaps? There were no more parties because we all had lost interest in each other.

Then, finally, the last breakfast. Goodbyes were said, addresses exchanged with promises to write, and we all embraced each other. The gangway connected us to firm soil. Another goodbye wave or two and each one of us started a new phase in our lives. Mrs Goudsmit had said goodbye to us earlier. The two male teachers had already grabbed a taxi. There was nobody there to meet Esther and her parents, and they stood undecided on the quayside, deliberating.

I stood at the railing waving a red cloth as arranged. A couple, Jaap and Annie, who were friends of Jan, greeted me extremely warmly.

"So you are Paula? Lovely to have you as our guest for a few days. Is that your luggage? Ok, let's go, Paula. The ship taking you to Borneo is moored over there, on the other side of the harbour. You'll be missing the *Christiaan Huygens*, because this other ship is really only a mail and provision ship that travels between the islands to serve the island population, and has only limited accommodation. But first you'll be introduced to our beautiful city of flowers, Surabaya."

The wedding

As I boarded the boat belonging to the *Koninklijke Pakket Maatschappij (KPM* – The Royal Dutch Steam Packet Company), my first impression was that it was some sort of Noah's ark: there were grunting pigs, cackling chickens, ducks, geese and all sorts of other birds in cages on board. The animals were walking around freely inside an enclosure in a dedicated area of the aft deck. A beautiful cockerel crept out from a basket, puffed up his chest and started to crow. I bet nobody would oversleep in the morning. Small native boys, stark naked but for woollen hats, fled back to their mothers who were busily chatting and conjuring up food from their baskets. Now I understood the smile on Jaap's face when he said I would no doubt be missing the *Christiaan Huygens*.

The purser came to greet me and said, laughing: "You do not need to stay here, madam. We have a very nice cabin prepared for you. Your luggage is there already. Shall I lead the way?"

Tea had already been served in my comfortable cabin and I could relax and recover my composure after all those unusual and new impressions.

Back on deck, I could not muster much enthusiasm for the scenery since the dark islands in the distance did not inspire me a great deal. On the contrary, I fantasised about Dayak headhunters; they lived in these parts, didn't they? Moreover, this Java Sea was anything but blue or jade green. In my imagination I saw an angry sea god busy churning the silt down at the bottom of the sea, turning the waves a dirty yellow. A thick blanket of clouds hovered over the sea, as if the sky and the sea were reaching out for each other, hankering for a fight. Suddenly a terrible thunderstorm broke and I was forced to flee to the small deck lounge where a fellow passenger started a conversation.

"Are you disappointed, madam? It usually happens like this, but when the sun is shining everything is different and then you would want to stay in the tropics forever."

"I do hope I will experience that. But why don't the children wear any clothes, yet have their heads covered, and with a woolly hat at that? At least the little girls are wearing dresses."

"Yes, perhaps you will find this interesting. Until around 1200, when the Muslims invaded this country, the religion of the population in this archipelago was Hindu. The many works of art and buildings bear witness to that. But after conversion most of the people became Muslim and that religion dictates that men and women have to cover their heads out of humility and respect for Allah, the All-knowing. It is just a few more days before the journey ends. I assume you are heading for Balikpapan?"

"Oh yes, my husband will be waiting for me there."

"Oh?" said the man, who had not even introduced himself to me. "I take it your husband is with the KNIL? I am an officer."

I replied spontaneously: "My Jan is still a soldier."

From then on, people stopped talking to me and the 'Officer' avoided me. Perhaps they have castes here, like in India. I thought of a Dutch Indies slang term I had already learnt: 'Soeda lama, Nonya' (never mind, leave it, lady).

The fourth day, day of our arrival! Radiant sunshine, a deep

65

blue sky, and even the sea no longer looked terrifying. I had been standing at the railing for an hour, ready to disembark, wearing a *Dirndl* dress, a traditional German/Austrian dress, and a large sun hat, which I had bought in Singapore.

The purser told me: "Be patient for just one more hour, madam. But you can already see Balikpapan over there, nestled against that hill."

"Is the bay so large then?"

"In this wonderful country everything is extra large. I hope you have enjoyed being with us on the ship."

He gave me a friendly look and said: "It would seem you have a long journey behind you."

Then, pointing at my lute he asked: "Will you be performing?"

"No, I'm not intending to. But, if I do, you are cordially invited."

"That's a deal. I wish you good luck, madam."

Then all of a sudden I spotted my handsome Jan on the quay, a little shy, or worried perhaps?

When I was finally standing next to him he said *"Guten Tag, Paula, haben Sie eine gute Reise gehabt?"* (Hello Paula, did you have a good journey?)

I laughed and answered: "Hello Jan, ja, *ich habe eine gute Reise gehabt*. And have you any other kind of a greeting for me?"

The ice was broken and, just as we had done in Amsterdam, we walked arm in arm towards our waiting car. It was so good to speak and hear my mother tongue again. The next day it would be January 12, 1939, our wedding day in Balikpapan in Borneo.

The bedroom door opened slowly. I immediately sat up on the edge of my large 'Indiesch' bed.

"May I come in, my dear?" I heard.

"But of course, Mrs Lanting, it is your house."

"Are you feeling a bit rested? I can imagine you must be a little tense after all those new impressions and I am sure that you haven't slept very well. I can't help thinking back to my youth in Friesland, and of course my own wedding day."

"I would love to hear more about that, Mrs Lanting."

"Look, here is your wedding gown. It's beautiful. The *baboe* (servant) has just ironed it".

"Mrs Lanting, may I ask you something?"

"Just tell me what you need."

"Do you have white orchids in your garden?"

"White orchids? My dear child, they have just been delivered. Follow me."

In the sitting room stood a young woman, holding a huge bouquet of exactly those flowers I had secretly longed for.

"I am Nanette and I thought that exotic flowers would be just right for you. May I call you Paula? Wait, I will also make a garland for you."

"To what do I owe so much love and friendship? I don't know how I can thank you."

"For the time being, a hug will do. Is that ok?"

And so I became the bride I had always dreamed I would be. Friends of Jan and the Lanting family had taken it upon themselves to make this wonderful wedding a great celebration. This would be a church blessing (the civil and legal ceremony had been the wedding by proxy in Amsterdam), and it would take place at four in the afternoon. Jan arrived and looked radiant, unable to say a word. He carefully kissed me as if I was made of porcelain. The church was at the end of the street called 'Bovenlangs' (along the top). We decided to go on foot. With their display of fiery red blossom, the hibiscus trees on either side of the street gave the whole scene a fairy-tale appearance. Further down, below the street named '*Onderlangs*' (along the bottom), I saw the KPM ship that had brought me here.

Scarlet hibiscus petals had been scattered along the aisle leading to the altar. The church was packed with civilians and soldiers. As we walked towards the altar the organ played a chorale from Handel's *Messiah:* '*Wie lieblich ist der Boten Schritt, Sie kündigen Frieden uns an.*'[12]

In a melodic voice the minister read a text from I Corinthians 13 verse 3 which talks about love. The last verse is as follows:

> '*And now abideth faith, hope, love, these three;*
> *but the greatest of these is love.*'

The final hymn '*Dankt, dankt nu allen God*' ('Now thank we all our God') was sung so enthusiastically by so many young voices that I felt very moved. After the service was over, everyone shook our hands at the church door and wished us much happiness.

During dinner at the Lantings something happened that on the face of it was unimportant, yet which still cast a shadow over an otherwise perfect day. Apparently I was not quite *au fait* with Dutch meal customs. When Jan asked me: "Would you please serve me, Paula?" I replied: "Oh Jan dear, just take what you like."

Mrs Lanting, who was keeping a keen eye on everything,

12 'How beautiful are the Feet of them that preach the Gospel of Peace, and bring glad Tidings of good Things' (from: Romans 10:15).

said in a rather too sharp tone of voice: "I think perhaps a Dutch wife is much sweeter to her husband than a German one."

I answered spontaneously: "Perhaps we should ask Jan that in a week or so."

An icy silence fell over the company and my face glowed red. What kind of silly thing had I said now? Luckily Mr Lanting saved the situation by bursting into an uproarious and infectious laughter and, turning towards Jan, said: "That's a deal, Jan. I will be knocking on your door tomorrow morning."

I hurriedly praised the spices saying: "I'd like to learn to cook like this, Mrs Lanting."

She felt obliged to make amends as well and politely replied: "Just come round whenever you like."

Jan said several times: "Well, have you ever."

After coffee and liqueurs we were taken to our new home. How wonderful, a house on stilts! It wasn't large but had a wide verandah at the front and a view of the bay with flowering hibiscus all around. About 150 metres behind the house was the edge of the rainforest. Red roses stood everywhere in the living room and bedroom, and there was a large box full of provisions to see us through the first week. I was moved by all this loving attention from Jan, the Lantings, friends and neighbours. I would be kept busy with visiting and writing letters of thanks and not forgetting many invitations.

Tempo Doeloe

My reverie during the long train journey from Surabaya to Batavia was cut short when the train passed over some points, making the carriage sway. The children slept on but Jan woke up.

"That house on stilts, Paula, did you really like it? I dreamt about it and reproached myself for not being able to provide anything better."

"Oh Jan, you don't know the half of it, I just adored it. Sitting there dreaming on the verandah with that view of the bay, an open harbour to the world, seeing ships come and go, all the activity of tiny little fishing boats and behind me the beginning of the rainforest. It all fuelled my imagination. In short you can compare my feelings with that of a child on *Sinterklaasavond*.[13] So, don't worry."

"And can you cope with the climate?"

"I think it will take a little while. To be honest, I thought that Borneo had something gloomy, something sinister with those almost daily and heavy thunderstorms, even though I must admit they did clear the air a bit. Any tree not standing in a protective clump was simply 'beheaded' by the storms, its bare, split, white branches pointing accusingly skywards. To me they seemed like tormented souls."

"Oh Paula, aren't you letting your imagination run away with you? It doesn't sound very Dutch."

"That may be so, and it is probably due to my profession, because when you deal with children you automatically start to anthropomorphise the most simple things. Children live in a world where every object is alive and moves. But as soon as the sun shone in Borneo, it was a paradise, with that wonderful '*kembang sepatu*' (hibiscus flower). The baboe brought me a branch of it each day."

"I really liked seeing you so enthusiastic about your new life with me."

13 The evening of December 5 when the Dutch traditionally celebrate the birthday of St Nicholas (whose history is closely intermingled with the stories of Santa Claus).

"What I really appreciated, Jan, was that you helped me in my desire to understand and learn about this country and its people. In the evenings you took me to the *pasar malam* (market). Little oil lamps would stand on the long tables, just cotton wicks in small tins filled with oil, and these small 'table lamps' would light up everything until the oil was burnt. You could buy all sorts of things there, like any market. A slight smell of decay wafted over the vegetables and fruit, and I felt that fleeting life and decay belonged to the tropics. Are you still listening, Jan?"

No answer. Why should he? My Jan does not care for too much talk, so I will continue my daydreaming.

One day we were allocated a 'common' brick-built house on the other side of Balikpapan, a very nice house with a garden. The surrounding hills were green but there were few trees, and I missed my house on stilts between the bay and the jungle.

Spread out against the hills were small kampong houses which, when lit up at night, caught my attention. Because Jan was away on duty so much, I was often feeling a little bored. So I was keen on exploring my new neighbourhood and getting to know different people.

The moon was so bright there was hardly a shadow to be seen. At the end of our street a path wound uphill, leading straight to one of the lit-up houses. I saw nothing wrong with taking a little trip up there, since I was used to solitary walks back home in Germany.

When I reached the lit-up house, the family – father, mother and three children – were sitting outside. They got to their feet as soon as they spotted me, the children hiding behind their mother's sarong. I just saw three pairs of big black eyes peering at me from somewhere. The conversation was pathetic. I knew too little Malayan and from their side came only some pidgin Dutch. I remembered a Malayan lullaby, which my *baboe* often sang, and started to sing: '*Nina bobo, kalau tidak bobo.*'(*Sleep baby, sleep*). The children appeared and the mother continued the song for I could not remember the words. The father offered *tubruk* coffee. When I left they all accompanied me for part of the way downhill and said '*Tabéh Nonya, selamat djalan*' (Goodbye, madam. Have a nice walk). What a delightful little adventure! But, when I told Jan he was livid. He was really angry, with worry I thought, which was sweet. He knew how afraid I was of snakes and therefore told me some horrible stories. Later on I learnt that snakes don't come out at night, but I still decided not to make any more of these trips.

Actually, I did things a decent Dutch woman would not dream of. There was a rain butt beneath the gutter. Whenever there was an evening downpour the rain filled the butt in no time at all, I would put on my swimming costume and take a dip to recover from the unbearable tropical heat. It was like a bath with a natural massage, very refreshing but unusual.

I also used to love going for rides in a *bedjak*, the means of transport used by the natives. It is a tricycle, quite comfortable, pedalled by a boy who, whenever he had to go uphill, would struggle like mad with the weight of his fare, so that you could feel his hot breath in your neck.

By the time I had finally 'adjusted' to my new life, I found out that I was pregnant. Jan had hardly set foot over the threshold when I called: "Jan, there is a little Jan on the way!"

"Great, but can we afford an extension of our family? I haven't had a promotion yet."

"What does that matter? I do not need any luxuries. We will be alright and I am over the moon!"

"Ah well, we will work something out and I would love to be a father. But how are you so sure it will be a boy?"

"Oh, I just know."

"I am happy really, but from now on you will have to take care, so no more antics or escapades and no more '*Haarlemmerdijkjes*'[14]."

"What on earth are you saying? We are not in Amsterdam; that is offensive."

"What do you mean with offensive? Now I think you haven't quite mastered the Dutch language yet. You are probably thinking of the *Zeedijk* in Amsterdam's Red Light district. No sweetheart, it is just an Amsterdam expression."

"Okay, Jan, I have learnt something else again, I am sorry."

"What about some coffee? I will get your lute and then we will have a nice sing-song."

Peace had returned to our new house in Balikpapan.

Our town boasted a Dutch *toko* (shop) that, once a month, sold provisions from Holland. It was very popular. One day Jan wanted to eat sauerkraut with sausage and bacon. "I really fancy that right now," he said. Since walking was supposed to be good for a pregnant woman, I went to the *toko* on foot to buy sauerkraut and the necessary ingredients. Oh, how gorgeous that sauerkraut smelled, really Dutch. I just could not keep my fingers out of it. On my way home I stopped at each corner of the street and took a mouthful. The contents diminished quickly, and by the time I got home there wasn't enough left for a meal. Jan

---

14 An Amsterdam expression meaning in this context 'a detour', but also has the meaning of 'talking argumentatively'.

found me crying at the table with only a little bit left on a plate in front of me.

"Oh Jan, I am so sorry, you won't be getting any sauerkraut. I have eaten it all on the way home." Luckily Jan could laugh about it and said: "Don't cry, we'll just have it some other time. But I'll tell you this; I will go and buy it next time, for I am not pregnant." I felt relieved and we went out for a meal at a Chinese restaurant.

Our little Jantje was born on December 17, 1939.

I was jolted awake and noticed that the moon had disappeared and a grey twilight was slowly creeping into our compartment, reminding us that morning was approaching. When the train passed close to the edge of the forest, something black slid past the window as if warning of impending disaster. I thought it was just my imagination playing tricks on me and pushed the thought aside. The rainforest retreated to make place for open land, with now and then a *kampong* vaguely visible in the dim light. It was so quiet that I once more felt at one with the rhythm of our train. Batavia was getting closer with each kilometre we journeyed. Batavia: I felt small snakes wriggling inside my stomach, gnawing at me and taking my breath from my throat. I was afraid, but did not quite know why or what of. Don't give in to it, I thought. There is nothing the matter just yet, and in the end things will go as fate decides. There is nothing wrong with being a little fatalistic at times.

Jantje turned over mumbling something and my Olaf produced a noisy little fart. It made me laugh and I thought: this is my reality, a lovely family. Let's be thankful.

"Jan, are you asleep?"

"No, but I heard you sigh. Is something the matter?"

"Everything is fine, I was just thinking back to our wedding. It was such a lovely day except for that little incident at dinner. Did you mind very much about that?"

"Oh gosh no, forget about it."

"I hope I can forget it."

"It isn't that important, we Dutch are just rather direct."

"Blunt, you mean," I parried. "Oh Jan, didn't we have a lovely time in Balikpapan with so many friends and acquaintances? Remember that '*Rheinische Mädel aus Köln*' (the girl from Cologne on the Rhine), the fair-haired Christel with her Jo from Limburg?"

"Do you really know how Jo happened to end up in the Dutch East Indies? He never talked much about himself."

"Certainly, Jan, Christel told me some of it. Jo was brought up as a Catholic and wanted to become a priest after completing his theology studies. He wasn't happy, and never told us why he had chosen to come here. He was a sergeant and did not want to be promoted."

"Yes, I know quite a few who have fled Holland because of the crisis and unemployment. But that Jo did not want to be promoted, no, I have never heard of that, although I did notice that the officers tried to bully him."

"I can imagine that they felt that Jo was far above them. Intelligence and narrow-mindedness don't go together very well. Do you remember when you were transferred from Balikpapan to Surabaya? When was that exactly?"

"I think it was January 1940. I was due to start a new training course in Surabaya. A lot of army personnel were being transferred then, including Jo who was with us on the ship."

"Ah, I remember now. We were both dreadfully seasick. It was

Jo who took care of our Jantje, who was then only six months old. When our Olafje was born in August 1941, we were living in Surabaya in a beautiful house with a garden. It was a wonderful time. Alas, we have never heard from our friends again."

"Well Paula, I don't have any good memories of those first months in Surabaya."

"Why not?"

"Have you forgotten they arrested me in May 1940 because I was married to a German woman? By then war had broken out in Europe and Germany had invaded Holland, which capitulated on May 10. The authorities here panicked and they started rounding up all Germans and anyone with any German connections. So, I was put in a Surabaya jail, because being married to a German woman was considered to present a 'serious danger to the country'. After three weeks they had to let me go, based on supporting documentation provided by friends and colleagues in Balikpapan."

"Oh, those weeks. Ridiculous! I was followed as if I were a spy. We had been living in an apartment you had rented for us and little Jantje. Mrs Jansen, an officer's wife who lived in the main building, had been very nice in the beginning, but when news came through that a Dutch fighter pilot was killed in an aerial dogfight, she suddenly became hostile towards me. She moved away and I was homeless, with nowhere to go for me and our baby son."

I thought back to that crazy time, and how, as if by a miracle, Mrs Derksen, who lived across the road, had come over to me and said: "I think it is dreadful what has happened to you, and would like to offer you my garage as temporary accommodation."

I knew that her husband had been a pilot also, and had been one of the first victims of the steadily spreading war. Shy and depressed, I had to fight my tears welling up and said: "Oh madam, I am so sorry about your husband, I...."

She replied quickly: "You could not help that; you didn't start the war, did you? Just come and stay with me until you find something better."

Turning to Jan again I said: "That's how everything was sorted out until you returned home after your arrest and you found us a lovely new house where we lived until now."

"Well, it was not quite like that, Paula. I completed my Officer training in August 1940 but was immediately posted to Batavia only to be sent back to Surabya several months later. I seemed to spend most of my time away from home. And here we are, Holland has declared war on Japan after the attack on Pearl Harbour and we are on our way back to Batavia where I have to join my coastal regiment."

A much longer parting was only just around the corner.

The twilight grey was growing paler. I could no longer keep my head upright and my limbs felt heavy as lead. The train continued its *boo boom, boo boom, chu chu, boo boom, boo boom, chu, chu* ... but I barely heard it...

When I woke up it was daylight already: the start of a new and noisy tropical day, with an abundance of sunlight and a clear blue sky. Jantje was sitting on his knees looking through the window, while baby Olaf closed and opened his little hands and accompanied his gestures with splutters and giggles. Jan had already taken down the cases and placed them in the corridor.

"Hello darling, were you able to sleep for an hour or so? As you can see, we are all set; just waiting for the train to finish the last stretch before we can get off."

There we were, on the platform in Batavia. My head was not as clear as I had hoped. Sitting in the taxi I looked back at the empty train. It was being prepared for the return journey to Surabaya: it was loading up coal and taking on water, and then other people would get in with their own thoughts and interests. Would those men and women with their children also be afraid of what was irrevocably on its way to *Insulinde*? How many of us would never make another train journey and would the '*Gordel van Smaragd*'[15] ever be as sparkling as it was right now?

War! In Europe that monster had been raging for nearly two years already. It was a catastrophe, although caused not by nature but by humans. We were deprived of news from our families in Europe. Living only from day to day, nobody dared to make any plans for the future.

The taxi stopped in front of a hotel. Above the entrance hung a notice 'Salvation Army Inn. Welcome!' In the lobby we were welcomed by a middle-aged lady. She wore a *sarong and kabaya* (traditional Indonesian long skirt and matching jacket) and had her grey hair fastened in a bun on top of her head. She looked at us with dark, beady eyes. Jan asked for a room for me and the children, as he would have to report to his army unit more or less straight away. He received an answer full of hate and contempt.

"We have no rooms for *Moffen*."

Jan took the cases and said curtly, with his face aflame: "Come!"

I had an image of nasty little snakes, wriggling up towards my throat, threatening to strangle me. It felt as if I had been put in my place for a second time, but now I knew what was awaiting me in Batavia.

15 Poetic Dutch name for Indonesia, meaning 'Emerald Belt' and referring to the many green islands that all make up Indonesia.

PART TWO

The House at Ampasiet

The world is weeping
Suffering is great
Hearts turn to stone
In blood and need

A soul wounded by war
will never heal
Whether friend or foe,
It's just the same

A child's soul oh so frightened
Lifelong nightmares
Powerless a mother grieves

But God will dry all tears
Of yesterday, today and tomorrow

Amen

Paula Kogel

Uncertain Times

Moving to Ampasiet A15

Lies opened the door. Half hidden behind her skirt a small boy, with exactly the same colour eyes as his mother, peeped out, looking from one to the other. They were warm, dark brown eyes. Lies said surprised: "Hey, hello Jan, it's been a long time! Unfortunately Jaap isn't at home. What can I do for you?"

Lies was a big, broad-shouldered woman with black hair, cascading down her shoulders from a middle parting. She looked at me and the two children. Then, when Olafje laughed at her, her stern face broke into a smile. She stretched out her arms and I handed her my little boy.

Jan explained what had happened to us in the Salvation Army hotel and asked her whether she could put us up for a day or two. She cuddled Olaf and said: "Come in, of course you can stay here. What horrid people, and they call themselves Christians; it is an utter disgrace." She cuddled the baby again before giving him back to me and went to the kitchen to make some coffee. Following her to the kitchen, Jan asked her if she knew of any landlords. Lies immediately rummaged through a drawer, saying: "If I am not mistaken, there should be an empty house in Ampasiet A. Here is the address, Jan. Finish your coffee and go after it straight away."

I thanked Lies for her friendly welcome and asked: "You were talking about Ampasiet. Is that the name of this neighbourhood?"

"Yes, this area is called Ampasiet, and the streets are called Ampasiet A, B, C, D and E. They are narrow and the houses are small, but comfortable, and mine is one of the smallest, so it will be a bit of a squeeze for now. But I am very glad to be of help."

"Thank you, Lies, I won't forget this. Look, Jantje and Nikki have made friends already." They were playing together in a corner of the room.

A little while later Jan returned and said: "I've got it! We have a house, and it is very close to you, Lies, at Ampasiet A 15. The landlord is a nice Arab. I have paid the rent for half a year in advance. Tomorrow the luggage and furniture will arrive. You only need to put us up for one night. What do you think about that?"

"Well done," said Lies. "You already displayed your excellent organisational talents a while back, in Balikpapan. You helped us a lot then."

Lies turned to me: "You see, Paula, when we lived in Balikpapan, Jaap already had a house and Jan was often our guest, so he became a good friend."

"Shall we go and have a look?" I suggested.

"Yes, good idea. You can leave the baby with me, but I'm sure that Nikki would like to come." Holding hands, the two little boys walked ahead of us.

Ampasiet A was wider than the other streets, and also

longer, I thought. A *slokan* (gutter) ran along the length of the street, an open sewer disappearing under the ground at the end of the street. A little bridge led to the front garden, which was fenced off by a gate. Three stone steps and a low wall led up to a front verandah. Stained-glass windows threw a cosy and intimate light into the front room. Ampasiet A 15 was a small semi-detached house with two bedrooms, each with a view of the garden. There was a large covered verandah at the back with a wall separating our part from that of the neighbours. The outbuildings were along a tiled path: bathroom, toilet, *gudang* (store room) and a kitchen. They bordered a nice garden whose focal point was a beautiful Japanese cherry blossom tree with wide branches.

Sometimes, when I enter a new building, I start to sniff the air, just as dogs do. What did I smell now? Happiness. I gave Jan a big kiss and said: "This is where I'll stay, whatever may happen."

"And, did you like it?" asked Lies when we returned.

"Oh yes, Lies, it couldn't be better. And you only have to put us up for the one night."

"Nice and close by, hey Nikki? You all go and relax and freshen up in the bathroom, Paula. It will do you a world of good and afterwards there will be a large *rijsttafel*[16] waiting for you."

Jantje and Nikki were already standing stark naked and had climbed onto a step next to the *mandi-bak*, a large tub for washing as there were no showers. They were cheering loudly as they tried to catch a carp with the saucepan you normally use for a 'shower'. The carp, of course, would not be caught, nor should it be, for its task was to eat any mosquitoes floating in the basin.

16 Literally, 'rice table' – a famous (now almost Dutch national) dish consisting of selected dishes of meat, fish, eggs and vegetables with different sorts of rice.

Removals were always very well and efficiently organised in the archipelago. They had to be, for there was a lot of moving around on the islands. Jan left early the next day to meet the coolies (native workmen), who stood waiting at our new house amongst the tea chests and furniture, and towards the evening everyone who could come, had arrived for the housewarming party at Ampasiet A 15. Lies arrived carrying a large bunch of hibiscus flowers, and wished us good luck in our new home. We were all sitting on the front verandah, tired but intensely contented, enjoying the blood-red evening sky and a cool breeze. Mrs de Ridder, our neighbour, came and joined us and added to the party atmosphere by bringing a bottle of wine. Alie, as she had introduced herself, seemed a level-headed Dutch woman. I estimated her to be in her early forties. Blond curls fell over her forehead, but they failed to hide her worried frown. She told us that she had not heard from her husband, a boatswain with the marines, for a long time now, and I could well imagine how anxious she was. As the red evening sky made way for a moonless night, our guests started leaving. Moths fluttered around the lamp. We extinguished the lights and longed for a rest after such an enjoyable, but tiring day.

In the morning Jan brought me a cup of coffee in bed. "To wake you up," he said. "You were restless all night, Paula. Did you have bad dreams? You kept on saying 'no'."

"Yes, Jan. It was a weird dream. I was standing in front of a railway crossing and there were lots of trains passing by. Each locomotive had a large notice on which the word 'NO' was written in large letters. What on earth would that mean?"

"Oh, I can explain that. It means: don't you dare move away. Just stay here. For the time being this is where you belong. When I have to leave, I shall take with me a mental picture of this house and you and the children, as a constant reminder for my return. But now I have to go to report to my section. I don't know if I will be getting any more leave. Just take care of yourself and the children."

He looked at the still sleeping children, and kissed me intensely and tenderly goodbye. Then he left, walking through the front garden, carefully closing the gate behind him, crossing the little bridge onto the road, and looking back to me once more. The way he left I will never forget.

Uncertainty and fear

My feeling of having found a safe harbour soon disappeared as snow in summer. It was nearly the end of February. In the tropics, the transition from one month into the next is almost unnoticeable so the weather is not such a talking point as in Europe. There the weather forecast inspires the first conversation of the day. 'What will I wear today,' we say, standing in front of the open wardrobe. 'How many degrees is it? Will there be rain, will the sun be shining?'

Here in our wonderful Dutch East Indies, however, we only wore light summer clothes, especially airy, flowing skirts, and sandals on bare feet. I loved it! The only downside was that everything had to be washed daily, but we had a *baboe* to help us.

February. I wondered how it was in Europe. Was it very cold there, or rainy? How long would the war last? 'God is with us' has been the motto of warmongering countries throughout the ages. Beautiful anthems are sung to celebrate our patriotism, but in a loud and aggressive way. For God and fatherland, Queen and country....

Wilhelmus van Nassaue, ben ik van Duitsen bloed.[17]
Deutschland, Deutschland, über alles.
God save the Queen
La Marseillaise

But what does God say? God is silent and thinks (according to me and perhaps I am wrong): "Sort it out amongst yourselves. You know what you should do, but you are all just like Jantje and Olafje, who ruin everything, but then re-build and say: 'It's much better now.' But you forget how cruel you are and what endless suffering you are causing."

Suddenly the air-raid warning sounded. Is this it? Has it begun? We had been advised over the radio to crawl underneath the bed whenever the air-raid warning went off. I did it once, lying amongst the mosquitoes. Never again! But Jantje loved it. At the first sound of the siren he would stick his little index finger up in the air and say: "Mummy, ai'pane, under bed." He would take his rag doll and stay under there, obediently, until the siren would end this ridiculous performance.

I wondered whether the children were sensing all this tension. They must have done, for Olafje cried a lot and was only happy when he was given a bottle. One day he was just lying there in his crib, fat and bloated. The doctor came, looked at him and said in perfect German: "*Er hat sich überfressen.*" (He has eaten too much)

I told him all this inner worry had given me severe constipation and he said '*Zwanzig Minuten sitzen bleiben*'. (Stay

---

17 First line of the Dutch national anthem: "William of Nassau, am I of German blood."

seated for twenty minutes.) Who on earth would have the patience? Twenty minutes on the toilet is an eternity.

Our GP, who must have had an excellent German teacher at his secondary school, was very knowledgeable in his profession. I had been suffering from anaemia caused by chronic amoebic dysentery caught in Balikpapan, and he prescribed an effective diet: stir fry 50 grams of raw liver together with garlic and *sambal oelek* (spicy sauce) for one minute in hot oil and add red rice and papaya. I would never forget that frying pan, and liver would never again be a favoured dish, but that diet did give me one advantage: I would enter the camp well fed and fortified.

New rumours

Uncertainty pervaded the atmosphere. The house on the corner opposite us belonged to Mrs Zandstra, a nice woman of Friesian origin. She had two sons who were always on the look-out for adventures. Every single day, around five o'clock, mother Zandstra would be looking for her boys, worried sick as we had been told by the authorities to keep our children near us. Yet, she knew exactly where her offspring would be hanging out. At the edge of the built-up area of our district was a medium high escarpment, where a small local train passed once a day. There the boys would be exploring, much too far afield.

However, this time Mrs Zandstra was standing in the road, with all our other neighbours, who were all watching the sky, shielding their eyes with their hands.

"Looking for aeroplanes?", I asked.

"No," they all said, "the sun has a ring around it."

Mrs Zandstra explained: "This is a very rare natural phenomenon. In Friesland we have a saying: "*A circle around the* moon, *nothing awry; a circle around the sun, many women and children will cry.*"

It was indeed a peculiar and pale sun, but Mrs Zandstra got all sorts of comments from the bystanders:

"Goodness, what superstitious claptrap."

"Do you really think it means something?"

"Oh, come on! You'll have us thinking the Jap will be on the doorstep soon."

"Well, that's not impossible, judging by all the rumours that have been flying about."

Someone said with great bravado "Even if the Jap does that, he will be chucked out immediately."

"Ah, the war will only take about three months, then the Americans will be here."

Ada Zandstra looked at me as if to say, 'We know better, best get prepared.' I said my goodbyes and walked back home.

People were, of course, only trying to hide their fears behind a self-assured exterior. There were regular air raid warnings but never any attack, and I thought they might just be Japanese reconnaissance planes.

But more and more rumours were doing the rounds, and at the slightest hubbub in the street, everybody would go outside to see what was happening. Curiosity always won over fear.

Big battle in the Java Sea – Many Dutch ships sunk – Among them, after a fierce battle, our flagship "De Ruyter".

Japs have landed in Borneo – Oil wells set alight.

Fighting in Surabaya – White workers on plantations tortured and murdered – Women raped.

The Governor, Baron Tjarda van Starkenburg Stachouwer, spoke over the wireless: "Fellow countrymen, please keep calm, nothing has happened as yet. Do not leave the city!" Yet the rumours persisted.

The battle in the Java Sea has cost hundreds of young lives.

In Balikpapan, decapitated bodies of workers from the BPM[18] are lying in the streets.

There was no end to the rumours. The plantations situated in the higher regions had supposedly been taken with brute force, and their Western managers and personnel shot or put on transport. Many white women apparently had been subjected to humiliating 'games'. All military personnel and other male civilians were said to have been captured and put on trains to the harbour of Tandjong Priok, for onward transportation by ship to destinations as yet unknown to us.

"Calm down, nothing has happened as yet!"
And the radio switched to lighthearted tunes, while the Japanese had set foot on shore.

How could the Governor tell us to keep calm with such wild rumours all around us? Despite his admonitions, many people had already left the city. Heavily laden they had fled in panic to higher ground. Did they know where they would end up? I would have no idea where to go, so I stayed on familiar ground: at Ampasiet A 15.

18 Bataafse Petroleum Maatschappij – the Dutch-owned Batavia Petroleum Company.

Orang Nippon

One morning I went to the *pasar* (market) to buy some fruit and vegetables. The sun was shining and the air smelled of spices, making each breath an aromatic delight. Birds sang and twittered, happy and carefree. During the night all the nocturnal animals had spent their energy and were now quiet and in hiding.

As I neared the market a totally different feeling took hold of me. There was a sense of foreboding and I felt oppressed and threatened by looming danger. Walking past the Chinese shops, I realised what was clouding the morning atmosphere. Normally, Chinese flags would be flying every day. I knew that and no longer paid them any attention. But today the Dutch flag had been replaced overnight by a white one with a blood red ball in the centre: the flag of the country of the rising sun.

I asked the stallholder: "*Apa ituh?*" (what is that), pointing at the flag. The man looked at me, with an air of pity as well as triumph, and said: "*Nyonya blanda* (white lady), if you have children, then go home, for *Orang Nippon*[19] will be here any moment now."

I quickly finished my shopping and rushed back home. Alie de Ridder was already on the lookout for me.

"Where have you been all this time? Come inside quickly and lock the doors."

So, what we had been expecting for so long, and yet had not wanted to believe, had finally happened. I tried to imagine Japanese soldiers. I did not have the faintest idea what they would look like. The street was deserted. Still, I was sure that behind each shutter blue and brown eyes would not miss a thing.

19 Literally: man from Nippon (Japan).

Then, they came. Nippon's heroes. A vanguard of small, stooping soldiers, wearing jungle shoes, guns at the ready. Nervously looking from side to side, they were quite ready to shoot at anyone or anything that moved suspiciously. Was that the army of the illustrious Emperor Hirohito? They did not look like heroes at all.

Jantje had opened the door. I quickly pulled him back inside. Too late, the man had already noticed me. He walked into the front garden, hesitated, and then knocked on the door. What should I do? Not open it and run the risk that he would kick the door in? I had to make a quick decision. Don't be afraid, I told myself, but of course I was terrified. So I opened the door. In front of me stood a Japanese soldier who looked well-groomed. Perhaps he was an officer. He bowed and, in English, asked for a glass of water. What on earth should I do now? I could not close the door, and did not want to walk away either, frightened that he might follow me inside. In the meantime Jantje had moved next to me, his wide eyes staring at the soldier's gun, just like all small boys all over the world would do. I had an idea.

"Jantje, this soldier is thirsty. Quickly, fetch a glass of water, will you?"

As quickly as he could, my little chap returned with a glass filled to the brim, spilling some along the way, and offered it to the man. He emptied it in one gulp and asked for more. Jantje apparently understood him, for he went to fetch another.

The 'enemy' told me that he too had a son in Japan, but with black hair and black eyes. He ruffled Jantje's hair.

"Thank you, madam, God bless you."

Once in the street he waved at Jantje and hurried on. I breathed a sigh of relief and thought: "Thank goodness that went alright."

Neighbours appeared in the street and came over. They had

observed everything carefully and wanted to comment on the event.

"Thank goodness that bloke has gone," someone said.

"You shouldn't have given him any water. He is the enemy."

"Why shouldn't she have given that fellow some water? After all, she is an ally, isn't she?"

I felt indignant.

"How could you say something like that? I have only done my duty as a human being while you all were cowardly hiding behind your shutters, waiting for things to turn nasty. Bah."

I went inside and slammed the door.

The first meeting with a Japanese had not been too bad. But it wouldn't be long before we would experience that not every son of this nation, so foreign to our nature, would behave as courteously and politely towards women.

And so, the rumours had become reality. Some women did indeed receive news from their husbands and many desperate women in our district got on their bikes and cycled past a train packed with Dutch men, faintly hoping to find a scrap of paper, thrown out of the train by their loved ones, bearing their name and a message. All the early excitement quickly changed into disappointment and doubt, and nobody had the courage to voice their dark thoughts.

Suddenly I received news that Jan's section had been captured and was being kept imprisoned in barracks in Tjimahi, near Bandung. If they wished, family members could apply for a pass to visit. So I went to a government building in Batavia and asked to see the civil servant dealing with identity cards.

A soldier took me to a room where a Japanese officer, who obviously belonged to one of the higher classes, received me with an air of kindness. With an inscrutable smile he asked me in good Dutch for the reason of my visit. He heard me out and then said that he would take my request into consideration and that they would let me know.

I waited for more than a week, but did not hear a thing. I refused to leave it at that, and, full of determination, I returned to see the same Japanese officer. He received me with the same politeness, but to my amazement he spoke perfect German this time and told me he had studied in Bonn. He promised I would receive the pass. I did not quite know what to make of this. I also did not realise how naïve my actions actually were. That would dawn on me just one week later.

One day the following week, when the last fiery red of the sun had disappeared behind the horizon, a *bedjak* stopped in front of my house. A Japanese officer dressed in khaki uniform got out and stood in front of my open front door. The children had just been put to bed. All of a sudden I recognised the friendly, multilingual civil servant whom I had visited twice. He greeted me and then apologised shyly for his unannounced arrival, but he had felt impelled to deliver news about visiting Jan in Tjimahi and to bring some nice and useful things for the children because we would soon experience shortages. In a flash I remembered that soldier from the French occupying army, all those years ago after the First World War, who out of pity for hungry German children had offered me a bar of chocolate. I can still visualise that bar of chocolate which I had refused then. "*Je n"ai pas faim,*" I had said proudly.

But what about him? This friendly son of Nippon? My female instinct sent warning signals to my brain.

"Sir, I thank you for the kind gifts and for your interest in our wellbeing but forgive me, I cannot accept your gifts." He looked so sad and disappointed that I started to feel sorry for him. He saluted, stepped into the *bedjak* and did not look back.

Jolande, my new Indonesian neighbour (Alie de Ridder had moved) looked over the fence and said "Now you have made a big mistake, Paula. You have abused a friendship and rejected his gifts. To an Asian that is the greatest insult."

I parried airily. "What? An insult? This gentleman speaks our languages and has studied in our countries. So he would have learned our customs as well. I am sorry, but I am sure he was thinking he had found a little girlfriend."

Jolande tried to defend him once more.

"Do you know what I heard? The women who are waiting near the barracks in Tjimahi, hoping to catch a glimpse of their husbands, are being beaten terribly and chased away with whips. He probably did not tell you that in order to save your feelings."

"So you would have accepted the gifts then, Jolande?"

"Oh yes! I don't want to insult anyone, not even a Jap."

At Ampasiet A17 lived a German called Karl Krämer who thought he ought to celebrate the alliance between Nazi Germany and Japan by drinking *"Brüderschaft"*[20] with the Japanese every single day until midnight. He took on an air of conqueror and drunkenly sang *Deutschland über alles*. Tongues were wagging about him in the whole neighbourhood.

It turned out that Karl had devised a drunken plan.

At midnight one evening there was a knock on my front door. I woke up and asked softly: "Who is there?" I did not want the children to cry.

---

20   Literally: Brotherhood – a German expression for drinking a toast with friends.

"Ich bin Karl Krämer, gnädige Frau. Bitte wollen Sie mal aufmachen?"[21]

I opened the door slightly and whom did I spot standing next to Krämer? It was the same Japanese officer who had taken such an interest in my children, but now a little the worse for wear.

Krämer acted as spokesman.

"Dieser Herr ist bei mir auf Besuch und fragte nach Ihnen. Dann gehen wir doch eben hin, hab' ich gesagt. Sie sind doch auch Deutsche, darum stehen wir hier."[22]

"How dare they!" I thought and said *"Stehen Sie hier, na dann können Sie ja wieder gehen. Ihr Herr versteht sehr gut Deutsch.*[23] And I can tell you this for free: if you wanted to be gentlemen, you would not have come and visited at midnight, and if you have anything to say, then come at a decent hour. In any case, I do not have *anything* to say to you." I softly closed the door and tried to get back to sleep, but sleep eluded me until dawn. I didn't see or hear anything from Karl Krämer again.

Francine

Those newly in power left us alone. We were able to come and go as and where we liked, they did not pay us any attention. Yet, it only appeared that way, as we had the feeling their eyes were following us wherever we went. The Japanese flag flew from all the important buildings. The radio station had been the first to be occupied. Now it only broadcast Japanese classical music,

---

21 I am Karl Krämer, dear lady. Would you please open the door?
22 This gentleman is visiting me and was asking after you. So, I said, let's pop over to see you. You are German too and that's why we are here.
23 Well, here you are, and now you can go again. Your gentleman understands German perfectly well.

something I delighted in although I would have preferred to hear Dutch ditties sung by Dutch people, instead of this Japanese music with its peculiar five-tone scale.

What was the mood like amongst the people around us? When I asked around, I usually received the same answer. "It could be worse. Just hope it stays this way."

And *that* was the hidden snag: if only it would stay that way.

There were no more overcrowded trains with men from the army or civilian posts leaving for Tandjong Priok. Most of the women stayed inside their homes and a visit to town was only seldom on the agenda. Although it was quieter in the Ampasiet neighbourhood, we became increasingly worried about the Indonesian youths. They were roaming the city, singing in groups, carrying long sticks, held like guns against their shoulders, and shouting *Merdeka*! (Freedom).

Every time they ran into European women their singing changed into terrifying and aggressive jeering. The atmosphere was filled with hatred.

Just before the invasion most of us had received our army pay for three months which meant that, for the time being, we were able to live without too much worry. Now however, with all the unrest among the population and without any certainty about the future, many of us were weighed down by anxiety and were no longer able to think positively.

"What will happen to us when the money has gone?"

"From whom can we expect any help?"

"Certainly not from the Japs. They'll just let us starve."

That was the sort of talk going round. It was obvious people needed comforting, and, as often happens in difficult times, many of them suddenly remembered there was a church where God lived who would never leave you. As a result all the churches were packed, to the delight of the clergy. Some of the women with many children who already were in dire straits, received support from the church, but now many families decided to live together. It would be cheaper, and people would be able to support one another. I was not altogether sure if I too really wanted to find someone I could completely trust. I loved my home, its space, and enjoyed being by myself. It often crossed my mind whether these plans gave the Japanese an idea. In any event, this would become only too stark a reality not long afterwards.

There is no such thing as coincidence. Either everything is predetermined or, what I personally prefer, our brain is attuned to send and receive impressions. For me, the latter turned out to be the case, because one day when I was out for a walk, I bumped into Francine.

"Hey, Francine, I did not know that you were living here as well. How is your daughter Mengsje?"

"Fine. I was just on my way to talk to you about something."

"Come along then, let's go and chat at my place. Is it important?"

"You know, Paula, that I can sometimes sense things way ahead of time, a sixth sense maybe? Well, I just feel so terribly worried about our immediate future, and I thought it would be best if we were to move in together. Between us we would be able to cope much better with all the misery, don't you think?"

"That's fine. Let's get things sorted out. You are welcome in my house."

I had met Francine in Balikpapan a few years ago. She had

followed her husband Willem from Staphorst, a village in Holland well-known for its pious inhabitants. Francine had arrived in Balikpapan dressed in traditional Staphorst costume. She must have felt so hot wearing those layers of skirts, the solid shoulder piece and a tight cap on her head. But by the time I was introduced to her she looked lovely in a flowery dress, with brown curly hair and blue eyes that looked straight at you. She was a woman you could trust in any circumstances.

My mind goes back to Saturday, December 17, 1939, the day I was due to give birth to my first son Jantje. I was in labour, having great difficulties, and we had not been able to get hold of the doctor. Europeans generally liked to party on a Saturday night, and everybody knew that the partygoers did not want to be disturbed by anyone or anything, no matter what, so someone had fetched an Indonesian midwife. That proved to be a life-saving decision because the umbilical cord had wrapped itself twice around the neck of my baby. If the birth had taken any longer there would have been a tragedy.

The following morning a woman stood in the door to my bedroom.

"I believe some help is needed here."

That was Francine. Practical and purposeful, she oversaw the situation and created order and peace in a jiffy. Afterwards, we had lost contact for a long time due to army transfers to other islands. But after this reunion in Ampasiet we very quickly became as one family with three children: Mengsje, Jantje and Olafje. We stayed together until the end of the war and shared joy and sorrow.

After the war we lived with our families in the Veluwe, a

beautiful part in Gelderland, the central province of Holland and an area of outstanding natural beauty, and kept in touch regularly. That is how I came to know that Willem had survived the horrors of the Burma railroad. Francine would have three more sons, but Mengsje died of cancer when she was nineteen years old. Mengsje, that quiet child with her bluish, transparent skin, sandy hair, freckles and legs as long as those of a ballet dancer. She walked as if she were floating on air.

Fortunately Francine was able to see her boys grow up before she died in November 1975.

'No flowers' it said in the death announcement. Was that considered a waste of money? Or just not done in orthodox circles? On her coffin was one large bouquet of autumn flowers, single proof of my love, friendship and gratitude.

Nippon becomes active

Until now the occupiers still had not put any obstacles in our way. Perhaps they did not know what to do with so many people. Our fear of Nippon seemed to fade somehow.

Then, overnight, everything changed. All the inhabitants of Batavia were summoned for registration, and the city was being divided into districts. Our district was intersected by a long and wide street, the Avenue Trivelli. Large houses with many rooms lined both sides of this avenue. One of the villas had already been requisitioned and refurbished as a Japanese office a while back, and a second one functioned as a hospital. For some time now we had been calling this Nippon house, situated at one end of Avenue Trivelli, *The Gate*. The district effectively became a camp, to be called Tjideng, although nothing had been fenced off as yet. Dutch men who had held certain indispensable functions were now the last ones to be interned and transported away. From now on the new occupying power would be in control of very many women and children, old men, doctors and young boys up to eighteen years old, and we knew what we could expect. 'Women and children are easily manipulated,' the new boss must have thought. 'They won't rebel.' This was the system of the infamous dictator. Apparently Nippon was scared to death of rebellion, riots and meetings, as well as religious gatherings. Whenever more than three of us stood talking together, one or two soldiers would hover close by, as yet quite inconspicuous, yet obviously present. So we held gatherings about religious questions in my house because the reverend's wife, who had originally organised such meetings, had stopped doing so out of fear.

As part of the registration process, everybody had to obtain a pass at *The Gate*. I received a German pass, along with the message that I was allowed to live in the town, outside the 'camp'. I now had a problem that only I could solve, without involving anyone, not even Francine. Being Lutheran, I was a guest member of the Reformed Church, and had got to know quite a lot of kind people. So I decided to visit Mrs de Vries who lived in a house in the town centre. 'I am sure she will be kind too and might give me some advice,' I thought.

After the usual greeting I explained my situation.

"Mrs de Vries, you must have heard what is going to happen. To the Japanese I remain German which means I will have to leave my house to live in town, although I fear that in the end all the European women will have to live inside the camp. That's why I thought that, until that time comes, I could live in someone's house in town, take care of it and guard it."

I had barely finished talking and instantly regretted I had

ever broached the subject. She gave me a look that could kill, then turned her back on me and looked out of the window. You could have cut the silence with a knife. A clock was ticking loudly on the dresser. This minute lasted longer than an hour. Mrs de Vries swiveled round sharply and with hate-filled eyes she spat out her reply.

"I'd rather hand over this house to a Jap than to a *Mof*. Here is the address of an Austrian woman who asked after you."

A bucketful of ice cubes could not have been colder.

Ignoring the note I replied: "Madam, I hope things will work out for you."

Cycling back home I had already decided I would never leave Ampasiet A 15!

The following day I asked for an audience with the Japanese mayor in Batavia. It was granted and I was allowed to come immediately. My curiosity once more overcame my fear. Stay polite, I admonished myself. A soldier led me to the room of mayor Nakama.

Seated behind an oversized desk was a Japanese official, looking more like a statue of Buddha than a conqueror of Java. His enormous belly drew my attention. That belly was almost split in half by the edge of the desk. A podgy hand with short, fat fingers calmly placed a fountain pen on the writing pad. He regarded me through small eyes, which looked like narrow openings between the hills of his cheeks and his wide nose. Those eyes did not emanate any evil. Rather, they reflected a feeling somewhere between good nature and boredom.

What language will he be speaking, I wondered.

"What's the problem?" he asked in English in a nasal voice.

My English was very limited and I only knew what I had learned at school, but I did my best.

I did not bow, for they had not yet taught us that. That would follow later, and rather roughly too.

"Excuse me, sir," I started. "I am a German woman, married to a Dutchman and I have two little boys. This area will be a camp for Dutch women and children. You gave me a German pass. Therefore I have to live outside the camp. The question is that I then have to rent a house and get work in order to provide for my family. Please sir, can you guarantee me those things? If you can, then I will go and live outside the camp."

He shook his head. He smiled so fleetingly that I did not feel very hopeful.

"I knew it, sir. So I ask you to let me stay here with the Dutch people. It may not be so easy for me to live among them, but that's war, Mr Nakama."

He still said nothing, so I continued explaining why I wanted to stay in Tjideng.

"I know Nippon is a successful nation that has conquered half the world. But there will, perhaps, be a time when Nippon is going to lose. Then *all* the European women must move into the camp. If I live in town and then have to move back into the camp, there will not be enough room for my family and me. I am sorry, Mr Nakama, honestly, that is what I think. I ask for my boys and myself, let me stay here."

He flew into a rage and tried to get to his feet but his huge belly was blocking his way. Waving his arms about and with flashing eyes he screamed:

"If you want to stay, stay! But I tell you, German woman, you shall see what kind of experiences will come to you, and to all the Dutch!"

He started to screech.

"You are wrong, woman! Nippon always will win. Have a look into the future and expect very bad experiences!"

He pressed a button and a soldier entered. A little later I was standing outside and I made a quick getaway. In my head thoughts and the words I had just heard were whirling round and round like autumn leaves in a storm.

When I got home, Francine was waiting on the verandah with the children. Even from a distance, I could see that she was worried. The children did not look exactly happy either, but when they saw me their little faces lit up. The sun was shining again on Ampasiet, at least if we can talk about sunshine, when literally and figuratively the sun was prevented from penetrating the big, dark clouds looming overhead.

The children were dancing around me when I stepped onto the verandah. Olafje was able to walk now and wanted to join in, but as soon as he lifted up one of his short, chubby legs, he lost his balance and landed painfully on his baby bottom. I played 'horse riding' with him on my knee and his tears were soon forgotten. Francine came in with mugs of delicious smelling coffee.

"Where on earth have you been yesterday and again today, Paula? I was so worried. Please tell me next time where you are going."

"I am here now, aren't I, Francine. Let's enjoy our coffee first. I will tell you all about it when the children go off to play in the garden. In any case, I will be staying here."

"What do you mean, staying. Did you want to move?" asked Francine, taken aback.

"Everybody had to collect a pass from *The Gate*. You got a Dutch one and I was given a German pass, which means that I really should have to live in the town. Last time, you told me that you were able to see into the future. Well, Francine, now I have had such a premonition."

I told her about my conversation with Mrs de Vries and the interview with Mr Nakama, the mayor of Batavia, and also about what he had said about any future experiences we may have in this camp.

"It all sounded rather threatening, Francine."

Francine listened attentively before she spoke.

"Just be glad that Mrs de Vries has refused you her house. What she said was of course pure stupidity on her part. You didn't cause any war, did you? And I have never felt at ease about the Japanese. We will just have to wait and see."

"Let's make a pact," I said.

"We've already done so," said Francine, "Holland-Germany; it can't get any better than that, can it?" she laughed.

"I am serious. Let's promise each other that, whatever may happen in this camp, under no circumstance will we lose courage, especially for our children's sake. Perhaps we should hold a little ceremony in which the children can be involved?"

"Wait, I will go and get them."

Jantje, Mengsje and Olafje stood between us, clasping hands. Francine and I placed our hands together and lifted them up high and repeated our vow twice: "We will survive, whatever may happen. May God grant us strength."

We remained silent for a few moments. The children too just stood there. Something sacred touched us all. I did not know how else to express it. We never mentioned it again.

Not long after this Christine paid us a visit.

"Have the children gone to bed already? Oh, what a shame. I would have loved to give them a cuddle."

Christine lived opposite Lies Matters. She was super slim, almost too thin, with frizzy red hair, freckles, and eyes that always seemed to laugh. She was a real sort of 'auntie', who was childless and could be seen daily with someone else's offspring in tow. This time though, Christine arrived with a different proposition.

"Do you also have the feeling that trips into town will soon be a thing of the past?"

"Quite possibly," answered Francine. "Were you planning an evening out in Batavia, Christine?"

"If only. Unfortunately I no longer have any money to spare for the cinema, but I still need to do some shopping. Who is coming with me?"

"If Francine can look after the children, I will," I said.

"I need to get some kapok and some wool."

"Oh, in that case, could you get me some gelatine?"

Our budgets were shrinking steadily. Therefore, Francine kept on buying huge quantities of fruit – at a good price, for she haggled like the best of them – to make a very tasty jelly she then sold to the neighbours, while I had started to make rag dolls, which I also managed to sell easily. The floppy dolls had green, brown, red, yellow or orange woollen hair. If Jantje had had his way, I wouldn't have been able to sell any of them, for he loved them all. I was allowed to sell his old doll though, because I had to wash that one daily and hang it out to dry. Not that difficult to guess why.

So, the next day, Christine and I mounted our bikes and set off for the town centre, to Koningsplein. We looked for the things we needed and treated ourselves to an ice cream. For one short moment, standing in that large, beautiful square near the white, sunbathed Governor's palace, we felt free. Then a group of POWs appeared, in rows of four and escorted on either side by Japanese, carrying guns with bayonets attached. They were not marching, rather the opposite. They were walking very slowly, but in step.

"Christine, there's Jan!" And off I went.

Christine called "Stay here, Paula. Be careful!"

A soldier pointed his bayonet at me and I stopped.

"*Saya punya laki, tua*,"[24] I said.

The soldier gave as answer "*Tida blanda nyonya, Australia.*"[25]

Red-faced, I walked back to Christine.

It made the Australians' day. They were grinning broadly, winked at us and some stuck two fingers between their lips as if they were wolf-whistling.

"But he looked just like Jan." I just managed to whisper.

Christine put her arm around my waist and took me home.

This was to be our last outing into town.

---

24 Literally: "to have a man, sir." In this context probably "I thought I saw my husband, sir".
25 "No, white woman, Australians."

Jantje (right) and Olafje, in Ampasiet A15, shortly before the start of internment.

Jan with Jantje on his wooden tricycle – Ampasiet A15.

Tjideng

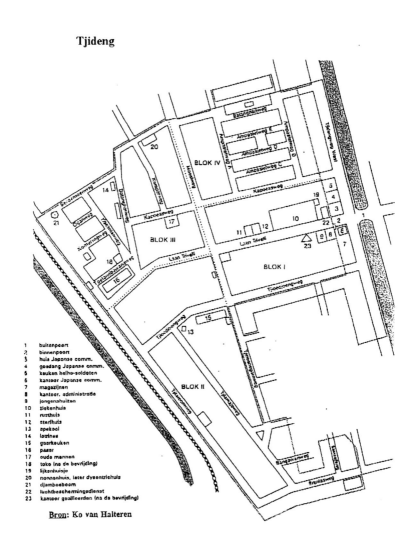

1 buitenpoort
2 binnenpoort
3 huis Japanse comm.
4 goedang Japanse comm.
5 keuken helho-soldaten
6 kantoor Japanse comm.
7 magazijnen
8 kantoor, administratie
9 jongenshuizen
10 ziekenhuis
11 rusthuis
12 sterfhuis
13 apekooi
14 latrines
15 gaarkeuken
16 pasar
17 oude mannen
18 toko (na de bevrijding)
19 Bjkenhuisjo
20 nonnenhuis, later dysentriehuis
21 djamboeboom
22 luchtbeschermingsdienst
23 kantoor geallieerden (na de bevrijding)

Bron: Ko van Halteren

Map of Camp Tjideng.
(Source: K van Halteren) – see this website for a clearer picture:
www.japanseburgerkampen.nl/tjideng/

110

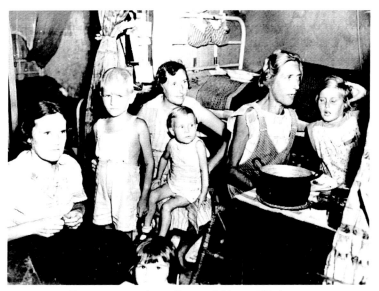

Everyone got their allocated 50cm in Tjideng,
(Source: Spaarnestad Photo, Haarlem, The Netherlands).

Tjideng – showing the deprivation the women had to endure.
(Source: Spaarnestad Photo, Haarlem, The Netherlands).

111

Map of Jakarta, showing Tjideng (now spelt Cideng) as a district of the city.

Camp Kampong Makassar, the camp where Roberte Swain-Halbertstadt, translator of this book, lived with her mother until liberation in 1945.

Japanese guards at the gate of Tjideng camp.

Standing in line for the meagre daily ration. (Ton Hardeman 2007)

Slamper, still young and in all his glory. Truly the 'best and most beautiful dog in the whole wide world' as we called him.

Paula with an aged Slamper and the mongrel 'Paljas' – the little rascal kept Slamper young and active for many years.

State of Tjideng towards the end of internment.
(Source: *Japanese Civil Internment Camps During the Second World War* –
original source unknown)

Jantje, after liberation of the camps, his oedema belly clearly visible.

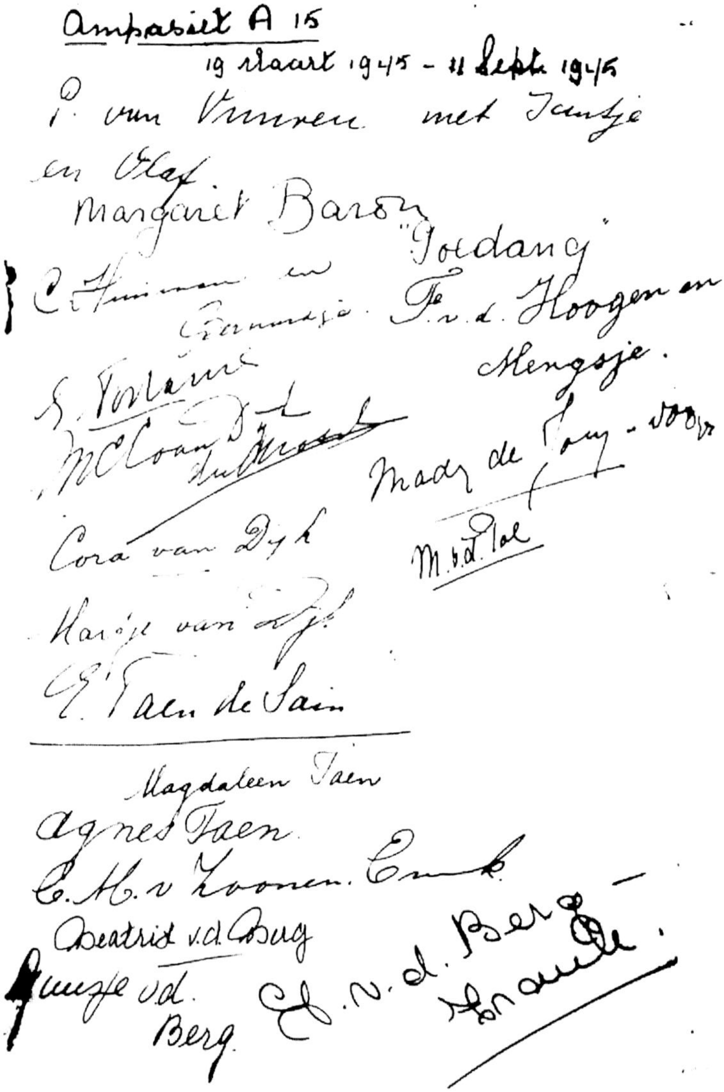

Ampasiet A 15
19 Maart 1945 - 11 Sept. 1945

(handwritten signatures)

Signatures of all the women and children resident at Ampasiet A15 in 1945. This is a copy from a Friendship book kept by Beatrix Taminiau (v d Berg), who was a teenager when she and her mother and sister arrived in Tjideng, among the last new housemates in Paula's house. She kindly sent this for inclusion in the book.

Behind Barbed Wire

50 cm

There was a nervous disquiet in the neighbourhood, and not only amongst the inhabitants; the Japanese seemed to relish whipping things up too. Soldiers, in groups of six, their guns and flashing bayonets at the ready, patrolled the perimeter of a camp-to-be. Posts and barbed wire were lying on the ground ready for the fencing to be built. The *gedèk* (bamboo matting) would be added later. Were we soon to be separated from the outside world? Was Nippon, behaving like the invincible conqueror, afraid that the women and children would protest? Fear overwhelmed friend and foe.

"We are going for a walk," Francine said.

"Mengsje, could you fetch the pushchair and put Olaf in it?"

"Olaf can do that all by himself," Mengsje said.

The sun had already passed its zenith, its soft rays shining diagonally across the rail track outside the still open camp. Two people, silhouetted against the light, were walking over the escarpment. We stopped. A Japanese soldier was pushing a young Indonesian boy in shackles in front of him.

Francine said: "Oh look. That is the boy who stole Mrs

Mertens' bicycle. She reported it and now they are going to chop off his hands. She cried when she told me. 'I wish I hadn't said anything. I am so sorry. He is still so young and all that for a stupid bike,' she sobbed."

We realised once more we had ended up in cruel hands.

Olafje climbed out of his pushchair and waved to the silhouettes on top of the escarpment.

"Da-da!" he called and picked a few blue flowers near a post lying on the ground.

Towards evening the following day the fencing was completed and Tjideng, the Japanese camp holding Dutch women and children, had become a reality.

Our average-sized district, with its mix of large and small single-storey houses, had now been completely closed off and was under the control of a camp commander with his staff and guards. To liaise between them and the internees, the Japanese had appointed a Dutch woman, who also had some staff reporting to her. The Dutch secretaries and typists felt privileged, I think. They were the only women who wore make-up and went to work well-dressed.

All 'volunteers' – women who had started to live together on their own initiative – had already found a space, but Batavia was a large city full of very beautiful villas surrounded by wonderfully landscaped gardens. In time all their owners would be forced to live amongst us, and Tjideng would become a very large camp for all the Dutch women and children. We soon discovered how this would be managed: we would just have to budge up.

Francine and I had already emptied the living room, and

had put some of the furniture in the garden. The dresser and the dining table, which were now standing outside beneath the window, made the garden look like an extension of the house. While we were busying ourselves with this, a slim, dark woman introduced herself to us. She was difficult to place with her black, tight-fitting clothes, dark hair and melancholy eyes. I thought her to be in her early fifties. She could be French, or might be of Indonesian parentage. Her eyes were so dark that I thought: 'I can't look into her soul.' She was called Mrs Fronté. She was grieving, you could tell. Yet she seemed to accept her fate courageously; after all, that's what we all had to face up to.

Mrs Fronté, who never told us her first name, spoke in a friendly, but aloof tone of voice.

"I have been allocated space in this house. Where would you like me to settle peacefully? I only ask for a space of 50cm."

She had a great, and at the same time very grim, sense of humour. Indeed, everybody would ultimately be allocated just 50cm[26] in which to sleep and store their few meagre belongings. In the end the word 'privacy' would be banished from our vocabulary.

I welcomed her and Francine said: "You still have a choice in our palace."

"Then I will choose this spot beneath the stained-glass windows since it looks nice and cosy. My son, André, will come in a minute to give me a hand, but he won't be living with me."

André, a handsome, tall boy of eighteen, arrived together

26 This was 50cm width and average body length. Although this would appear an impossible space, it is a fact that the Japanese camp authorities allocated such strict living space to all prisoners, and there are many comments about this in the various books written by survivors. Paula and her fellow housemates appear to have had a little more space available than average, until in 1944 the camp came under military control and conditions deteriorated rapidly.

with a friend of similar age, carrying two trunks. They placed these beneath the window in such a way that enough space was left for a basket full of kitchenware. Then they placed a plank on top of the two cases and, on top of that, a single mattress.

"This is my personal hotel suite," Mrs Fronté said cynically.

The boys left immediately to help other women. They had been allowed to borrow a two-wheeled cart from *The Gate.*

Over a cup of coffee, Mrs Fronté's frosty attitude melted and she began to talk. Fortunately we had not yet had to give up our coffee, since we had stockpiled a great deal before the closing of *The Gate.*

"You make a lovely cup of coffee," she started. "Do you mix various kinds, such as Arabian and Java beans? Do you know how to brew the most delicious coffee?"

"No, please tell us," I replied.

"You need to start at eight o'clock in the morning by putting the coffee, well covered, on ice cubes to allow it to percolate. Then at ten o'clock, you have the best coffee in the world," explained Mrs Fronté.

"I'd like to try that some time," I said.

"That's all very well what you two are talking about, but where are we going to get ice cubes? Even if we still possessed an ice box, we would have burnt it ages ago."

That was Francine all over, always practically minded. We had to laugh and forgot that there would come a time we would have no coffee at all.

Mrs Fronté fetched her photograph album and showed us what she had had to leave behind: a villa with a wonderful garden, which had been her hobby. I understood her grief for the loss of such a piece of paradise. I felt that I would feel the same should I ever have to leave this small house at Ampasiet A.

She continued: "I am very worried about my husband, who has been interned. He is no longer as young as he used to be and he has a heart condition." She did not look up while she was telling us this, instead drawing circles in the sand with the tip of her shoe.

"You have already met my son André. My other son is with the Marines. I am so scared."

"Mrs Fronté, we are all scared. But you mustn't be afraid of things that haven't happened yet. If we worry like that, we will never make it."

"Maybe you are right." She pointed towards the children playing.

"Do the children still remember their father?"

"Mengsje does," said Francine, "but Jantje and Olafje are too young."

"You must tell the children as much as you can about their father. If he returns, they will at least have something in the way of a common memory," Mrs Fronté urged. "What do you expect will happen?"

"I don't expect anything," I explained. "We have switched off the past, up to a point. We are living in the present, from one day to the next."

"And the future?"

"Francine and I have solemnly promised each other that we will survive and we've asked God to grant us strength. That's how we live our lives at the moment."

Francine nodded in agreement.

"I am often struggling with questions to which I cannot find an answer," Mrs Fronté said.

"They say that if you trust in God, everything will be alright. I am asking you: what if it won't be alright? What happens if the people that I love don't come back?"

She had to swallow before she could continue.

"Then they will say that it is God's will. What do I do with such nonsense?"

I could feel her despair.

"Francine, what do you think about such fundamental questions?"

"What do I think? I have had a religious upbringing, so for me it will be God's will, whatever may happen. But I'd like to say that I do not really feel alive when my Willem is not with me. Maybe that is a bit of what Mrs Fronté means?"

Our housemate nodded tearfully.

Now it was my turn. What should I say? What did I actually think about these questions, despite my belief in God?

"I am also humbly searching for answers to these questions, which occupy each and every one of us in these awful times. I think that, to make life simpler and more bearable, we could look at it from a different perspective. We are all totally possessive about anything we receive or forcefully make our own: it becomes ours alone, because we have worked for it or paid for it. My husband, my children, my family, my house, my surroundings, my money, my clothes and my jewellery; all of it is mine. Sometimes people even go as far as considering their friends their possessions. And we all know it always goes wrong. In my experience, thinking back to my own country during and after the First World War, all that you have ever valued can be taken away in an instant. And that's exactly what is happening again now."

"I can understand that," said Mrs Fronté. "I know it is not easy to say goodbye to prosperity, although it is not so bad if wealth stays in the family. But what does God have to do with it? Is there some being above us, some sort of a power or force that determines our fate, or manipulates us, or that just influences our lives, our thoughts and deeds? Could you explain that?"

"I can only explain what I myself feel, think and experience, and I am always willing to learn from others."

"I would like to hear more," Mrs Fronté indicated.

Francine had apparently had enough of this.

"Why are you all making it so difficult when it is so simple? I hope you manage to find a solution. I am taking the children for a walk."

Mrs Fronté smiled and said she envied Francine's self-assurance.

"Perhaps we are indeed making it too difficult. We'll talk about it some other time. I am going out for some fresh air too."

I was glad I no longer had to carry on trying to explain things. Actually, I did not feel like delving too far into my own soul either. Let us all just live and survive; that alone would be quite a feat right now.

That same week we welcomed two more ladies into our house, who made their own 50 cm look quite 'cosy'. A tall and thin woman introduced herself as Mies. She never spoke much but, every time she saw us, would always give us a friendly smile. She slept in the house, took care of herself as much as she could, but would then disappear for the rest of the day. Annette, sandy-haired and still in rather good shape[27], was more talkative. She told me about her marriage, which did not seem to have been so rosy, as she had been subjected to physical abuse.

A week later another woman joined us. She called herself Babs. In better times Babs had been quite a large woman. As we

27 Over time new arrivals in Tjideng would come from other camps, usually emaciated and exhausted. The Japanese were forever moving prisoners from camp to camp. They did the same with the POW and male civilian camp inmates.

were increasingly put on a 'diet', Babs had lost weight rapidly. Now her skin hung around her in loose folds. Poor Babs.

Francine said: "Ah well, we are still young and may recover later, when this nightmare is over."

"And when will that be, Francine?"

"Just wait, Paula. That time will surely come – and perhaps unexpectedly."

Singing

It was still possible to go to the *pasar* every morning. The three children came too, Olaf in the pram, while Mengsje and Jantje were walking ahead or dancing around me. They had great fun. Once, when we returned home, I discovered a packet of butter and some eggs on the kitchen table.

"Oh look, Jantje. The fairies have been." Straight away Jantje and Mengsje started to sing *Op een grote paddestoel*.[28]

Francine was not at home, so I asked Jolande whether she knew who had surprised us with these items we only rarely could afford. Jolande said it was a secret.

"Come on, Jolande. That's not fair. I would like to say thank you to that person."

Jolande gave in and told me: "They were the two ladies who have moved into Krämer's house. They said that, if you insisted on knowing who had left such kind gifts, I should ask you if they could come and join you on the evenings when you are singing your songs and playing your lute."

"Who are these ladies?"

28 'On a large toadstool, red with big white stipples' - a well-known Dutch children's song.

"All I know is that they are two Jewish sisters from Antwerp."

As soon as Francine came home I went to number 17 to say thank you. It seemed they were expecting me. They introduced themselves with a sweet smile and said that they were called Ruth and Anna. Ruth, who was the younger of the two and a live wire unable to sit still, began to speak.

"We have been in Batavia now for several months. After having sold up in Belgium we managed to catch the last ship from Antwerp. We have been living in a hotel but they closed it down. Luckily we could rent this house."

Anna cut in and told me how much they wanted to sing.

"We have heard you singing on your verandah and we would love to join you. We still know the songs from our schooldays."

Because I had seen, back in Germany, what was happening to the Jews in Europe I was glad that I could give them some joy.

"Lovely to have met you, Anna and Ruth. Please come along, my house is always open to you. The more singers the merrier."

When I came back home, I said to Francine: "I hope they will be alright. They are festooned with jewellery. I think that's very dangerous."

"Yes," said Francine. "It would have been better if they had sold everything, but sometimes it is difficult to let things go. Maybe some of the pieces of jewellery are heirlooms or they are keeping them for a rainy day."

So they came and sang with melodious voices and they were happy. Ruth and Anna were always smiling. They never mentioned the war in Europe, nor did they ever talk to us about their own lives. Sometimes I tried to start a serious discussion, but it was impossible. They maintained a generic and forced cheerfulness.

We had been singing for a month or so and more singers had joined us. This is how our house became a meeting point. More and more people wanted to participate and we sang and played daily and my lute was put to good use. The house was always full.

Then a Japanese soldier arrived.

"What kind of meeting is this?"

"We are singing."

After that we were only allowed to sing twice a week, on Wednesdays and Saturdays. In any event, the monsoon season was approaching and our get-togethers became fewer and farther between.

Suddenly number 17 was empty. Ruth and Anna had gone. I asked the neighbours up and down the street, but nobody had seen the sisters. I began to suspect the worst. The Japanese had surely taken them away, I thought.[29] Francine and I were shocked, and I was furious about such injustice. It made me very sad.

"I shall go and enquire," I said. "They just can't do that!"

Francine stopped me.

"There's nothing you can do, Paula. You would only be making problems for yourself. Each person has his own cross to bear. And, don't forget we may be in for a very long haul."

I agreed with Francine and resigned myself to the situation.

29 "The Japanese were more anti-Western than anti-Jewish. Yet, anti-Jewish propaganda did appear, especially in Java, and by the end of 1943 most Jews had been interned with the allied nationalities, but were kept in separate groups. By the end of the war, however, they were all mingled with non-Jewish internees." From: *De Japanse Interneringskampen voor Burgers Gedurende de Tweede Wereldoorlog* (*The Japanese Civil Internment Camps During the Second World War*) by Dr D.van Velden - 1985, Uitgeverij T Wever BV, Franeker.

That night I dreamt that I was standing with my mother in the market square of our town, both watching powerlessly as the Jews were loaded into lorries and taken away.

Kumpulan

The Japanese occupiers wanted to know exactly how many 'rats' they had 'trapped', and that meant *Kumpulan*, the daily count or roll call, despite the fact that internees continued to arrive in the camp, making the counting a nightmare. Some of the squares between the streets were allocated for this twice-daily roll-call.

"That's going to be our daily 'outing'," I said to my housemates.

This roll call involved bowing for the enemy, out of respect. We had to gather at eight o'clock in the morning and at five in the evening, in rows of five, together with the children. Initially, the children thought of it as a joke and turned the bowing into a game. That soon stopped when their mothers were beaten, and we kept a sharp eye on the children.

Then came the command: "*ki wo tsuké! – keirei! – naoré!*" (attention – bow – stand up) and that sometimes repeated five times in a row. Writing this down I again feel the humiliation and the shame deep inside my bones. We had to bow at an angle of precisely 90°. If we were out, we would learn the hard way. A tallish young woman, standing in front of me, was slapped in the face every day. We could not understand why she was being punished. I went to have a chat with her and that's when I noticed that she had a permanent smile on her face. So the Jap must have been thinking that he was being laughed at twice a day! From then on we placed her a few rows towards the back, behind an even taller woman.

One day we were told that we had to come to *The Gate* to hand in all cameras, in person. So we set off to our 'Master' carrying our expensive, cheap or even useless cameras. The villa had a flight of steps on which the staff stood waiting for us. In front of the house was a large, well-cared for, circular lawn. We had to walk around this in single file, like geese, and lay our cameras on the steps at the feet of those in power, turn around towards the soldiers and bow. We had been taught how to do this by now. Three times we had to walk around that lawn and three times we had to bow. The intention was to humiliate us and, after having bowed for the second time, I thought: 'No more, not for a third time.' I looked straight at our rulers, not in an unfriendly way, but I did not bow. They can do only two things, I felt. They'll either haul me up the steps and give me a beating, or they'll just ignore it. I was nervous about what might happen. But then, a tall Japanese officer ended all the bowing with a wave of his hand. It was the same officer who, in the beginning, when I was still singing Mozart, Schubert and Brahms lullabies on my verandah during a full moon, had come to me with music sheets to copy down *"Schlafe holder süsser Knabe"*[30] so that he could send them home to Japan.

There were also raids for what the Japanese deemed to be unnecessary possessions, such as suitcases with stuff nobody really needed. After all, there was a war on and the losers just had to be grateful for their lives and for being given the minimum that they needed to stay alive.

This time, my *gudang* (store room) too, full of suitcases, was emptied. Each 50cm of space that was available needed to be used. The suitcases were chucked onto the street and the sixteen

30 'Sleep, dearest sweetest little boy.' From Cradle Song by F.P. Schubert (1797-1828): "Wiegenlied" – opus 98 nr.2. Words attributed – perhaps incorrectly – to Matthias Claudius (1740-1815).

to eighteen-year old boys pressed into collection service. A flat cart served as a rubbish cart with the youthful collection gang as personnel.

Suddenly, everybody rushed outside. The sound of delightful, carefree laughter rolled through the streets of the camp, like waves breaking on a North Sea beach. Nobody knew what was happening and we waited impatiently for the waves of laughter to reach our street too. Then they came. No refuse collectors in working gear, oh no, definitely not! 'Ladies' in evening dresses and long gloves, the dresses ill-fitting and hanging somewhat loosely in those strategic places that should be filled out... The 'ladies' had long, thin arms and legs, and walked barefoot or in sandals. But the beautiful hats with wide brims decorated with flowers were a marvellous fit. How lovely, to be able to laugh with such gaiety. Stately and self-assured the 'ladies' went about their task. Street by street they went, piling the suitcases up high on the cart, which needed to be pulled with increasing effort. They trod on the hems of their beautiful silk evening gowns when they bent forward. It was such a funny sight. But when we stopped laughing we worriedly thought: "Hopefully that will end well."

What had happened? Being curious, the boys had opened the cases and had given themselves and us some carefree fun. We will never know whether they visited all the streets. At the end of our street in Ampasiet A we discovered how absolutely humourless and ruthless Nippon was, and how nervous. Nobody laughed anymore and hatred was reigning supreme. The sound of whips hitting the naked backs of our boys, who had only wanted to have some fun, was heard far and wide. Disappointed once more and filled with sorrow, we went back indoors to our 50cm.

Else

After the closing of *The Gate*, it had become impossible to obtain vegetables and fruit. The little gas lights burned only a few hours a day. Working to earn some money was no longer possible, and I could only finish those dolls that had already been ordered. Francine was unemployed because she had to cease her jelly production, and we had only a few pots of jelly left for our own use. Determined, Francine looked for other work, and eventually went to do the laundry for Mrs Serkius who, together with her fifteen-year-old son, lived across the road.

Mrs Serkius was Jewish. She spoke a little Dutch, but excellent English. Her small, round figure was in continuous motion, which was further reinforced by her constantly moving hands, for she was in the early stages of Parkinson's disease. With her friendly smile, she loved chatting to the neighbours. To earn some extra money she taught English to those who were interested, and could still afford it. Ed, her fifteen-year-old son, had long, gawky arms and legs, and never did anything useful to help his mother. In fact, nobody knew for sure whether he actually was her son. Mrs Serkius loved talking, but never about herself. We had no idea where she came from; England, America or wherever. Her face never showed any emotion. She was just a friendly woman.

Francine had been doing the laundry for the two of them for several weeks when, one day, she furiously said: "I no longer want to do the laundry for Mrs Serkius. That son of hers makes me so sick, the way he hangs around all day and just leaves his dirty clothes all over the place. Bah, I am looking for something else."

"Oh Francine! That poor Mrs Serkius with her illness. What will she do?"

"If you feel sorry for her, Paula, then you go and do it, for I shan't!"

"Me? How can I? I still have all my dolls to finish."

Francine still had not calmed down and said: "That kid, that Ed, will have to learn to use his hands properly and do his mother's washing for her."

In the street we bumped into Christine. She stopped us and said: "Ah, good, you are here. I have something to tell you."

"Good or bad, Christine?" asked Francine.

"It's not camp news. That is always bad. It's just news, and it is about those down there. "

"Who are 'those down there', Christine?"

"You know surely. They are Elli and her friend Herma."

"What's with them?"

"They have male visitors nearly every day."

"They are welcome to them, Christine, if they like their visitors," was my comment.

"But don't you get it? Male visitors these times can only mean Japanese."

"Don't discriminate, Christine, a man is a man."

"Well, we will soon hear what might happen."

Christine seemed a little disappointed at our reaction. Whilst walking along with us, she excused herself, saying: "I have an appointment. See you."

"Surely not with a Japanese, Christine?"

"Do I look like I'd do that?" she laughed.

"Those down there won't have it easy," Francine said.

After a detour along the escarpment, we went home to find a notice announcing yet more new housemates.

As evening drew near we welcomed two ladies with their luggage, carried by two young girls from the staff of our liaison officer and organiser, Mrs van Voorst. They introduced themselves. "I am Bertha van Briel, but you can call me Aunt Bertha. This is my friend, Mrs Baron. She does not speak any Dutch. That should, I hope, not be a problem, for she has me as her mouthpiece. I will promise to translate her English faithfully."

Mrs Baron looked typically English: reserved, kind and polite. She mentioned she could play the piano and, of course, I stored that snippet of information away. Other than that they never said a word about their backgrounds, and did not ask about ours either. Aunt Bertha came across as much more cheerful and with a sense of humour. She was small and very lively and was always there when there was something to laugh about. Her laughter would often bring a lot of joy into our house. As if they had studied a map beforehand, they walked straight along the tiled path to the *gudang*. The *gudang* was small with a narrow opening in the back wall for light and ventilation. The girls helped them with their beds and luggage and then disappeared through the garden.

This budging up or 'downsizing' continued apace, but our house had not yet been filled to capacity. Francine and I could still withdraw to our bedrooms. Not long after, however, two of our housemates left to live somewhere else, but we immediately received replacements: Joop and Nel, with Bernard, Nel's two-year-old son, who were to stay with us until the end of the camp period. Joop and Nel took over Francine's bedroom, and Francine and Mengsje moved to sleep in the living room. All the changes happened without much fuss, and nobody grumbled or showed any kind of discontent.

Joop, a large woman with a friendly face, enjoyed making herself useful for our small community. She often brought something back from her walks, to the benefit of us all. For instance, a bag of charcoal she had found, or wood for our communal fire in the garden, where we all cooked our meals – for the gas light had long since given up the ghost – or water for our tea.

Nel, a tall, slim woman, was friendly but had sad eyes, which would often stare into the distance. She had been evacuated from Balikpapan, together with other women and children, before the Japanese had landed. She told us that her husband and many others from the *BPM* had been beheaded after the oil wells had been set alight. So the rumours had been true after all.

Due to all the new arrivals in the house, we had forgotten about Mrs Serkius. When things calmed down a little we saw different people in her house.

"Francine, have you seen Mrs Serkius and her son?"

"No, I haven't given them a thought lately. Are there other people living there?"

"Yes, I saw five mothers with small children in the front garden."

"Then Mrs Serkius and her son are sharing Ruth and Anna's fate. Oh, how awful."

That evening we went to bed feeling very sad. Suddenly, in the middle of the night, I was woken up by sounds coming from outside. Then I could hear it quite clearly. It was someone cursing in what was clearly a Viennese accent. I got up and quietly I walked towards the tiled footpath. From there I could see who had disturbed our night's rest: they were my Viennese friend Else and her daughter Erika, the Swiss Herta and Anna from Beiern, together with two other women with their children I did not know. They were each dragging a suitcase, a basket, a bucket and a thin rolled up mattress. She told me a few days later that, despite having Austrian nationality, she also had to move into the camp because she had married a Dutchman. So, all the other European women were sent into the camps after all. It had happened within a matter of months, much earlier even than I had expected. Mr Nakama, if I ever get to speak to you, I hope that you will agree with me: "Nippon will soon begin to lose!"

After the war, Else and I gave many concerts. She could play the piano and was always ready for a party, where she would accompany me while I sang Viennese songs with great gusto. Else is now 93 years old. She did not have it easy in the camp and now suffers from glaucoma – a heavy punishment for a pianist – and is nearly blind.

The hospital

The little house at Ampasiet A had to cope without me for a few days, for I was lying in a hospital bed beneath a large window in a house that was serving as a surgical hospital. The 'hospital' was close to The Gate. The Trivelli Avenue, the wide, main street of the camp, was lined with houses similar to the hospital, all surrounded by beautiful gardens. I had been admitted with tonsillitis after my housemates had unanimously urged me to go.

"Have those nasty things removed once and for all, while it is still possible. We will look after your children. Who knows how much longer we may have doctors in the camp. Dr Flits is an excellent ENT doctor, so get on with it."

Twice a year, ever since my childhood, swollen and infected tonsils had indeed been making my life a misery. So there I was, lying in bed watching my fellow patients, the nurses and the doctors. It was very crowded, for the rooms were small. Many villas, such as this one, had been terribly neglected since the district had been turned into a camp. The walls were no longer whitewashed, the *djati* (teak) panelling no longer oiled and the floor tiles looked grey instead of a shiny black. In the past – how long ago was that? – when the mistress of the house would still have a staff of native servants at her disposal, the house would have been filled with a pleasant air of freshness and cleanliness.

A paradise: at six the sun would rise, children and pets would be cavorting in the grass covered with dew. Using a *kipas*, a small hand-held fan, the cook would fan the flames of the *arang* fire that would start to smoke in the damp morning air, the smoke trapping an abundance of tropical smells. The lady of the house, dressed in an elegant morning gown, would invite everybody to the breakfast table. The smell of coffee and home-made bread would mingle with the fragrance of freshly cut, dew-fresh flowers standing in large vases, picked by the gardener every morning from a well-tended garden, before the heat of the sun became too much.

After breakfast the father would take the children down to the bathroom, where they would 'shower' using saucepan-like implements filled with cool water from the *mandi*-tub. Usually the kids would make great fun of trying to catch the carp kept in the tub to keep it clean.

The father would then start the car, call the children and take them to school before proceeding to his own place of work in a cool and simply furnished office. The mother would walk with the cook to the market to do her shopping. Everything was fresh and cheap. Such was the daily routine. The other staff would leisurely start their housework. Why hurry? When you are living in the tropics, it makes no sense to rush things, but to go about your business as calmly and quietly as possible. After all, tomorrow will be another day.[31] The war had put a cruel end to this idyllic way of life in the tropics. The atmosphere of the good old days – *tempo doeloe* – had disappeared. It had been a way of life that was never to return. The wound, caused by this war, would ache and bleed for a long time until a new time would arrive that would begin to hide the scars.

I sighed and became aware of Dr Flits standing next to my bed.

"You were very far away, madam, for I have been standing here a while. Where were you with your thoughts? Was it nice there?"

"Yes, as nice as a fairytale."

"They probably did not have any wars there pulling whole families apart? How do you feel, madam? If you have a cold I won't be able to operate."

"I feel fine, doctor. I don't have a cold."

"Then we'd better start, beginning with 'nil-by-mouth'."

He wanted to leave but turned back once more and whispered: "Just look at nil-by-mouth as a little practice."

"Don't spoil me too much, doctor!" I called after him. He laughed and turned to another patient.

The operation was planned for 10am the next day. Suddenly everybody rushed excitedly towards the window to see what was

---

31 Note from translator: "This reminds me of an expression often used by my mother "plahan-plahan", literally meaning "slowly-slowly."

happening in the street. I lifted myself up a little and saw a troop of Japanese soldiers running at the double through the street. I fell back on my pillow again and asked my fellow patients standing around my bed to tell me more.

Grete looked white-faced and her legs were trembling. She had just given birth to a son. A nurse wanted to take her back to her bed but she refused.

"I'll sit on Paula's bed if I may, but I must see what is happening outside."

Grete had been in the camp for a month. The Japanese had shot her husband at their plantation in central Java as he had not handed his keys over quickly enough. Trusted and faithful servants had secretly taken the heavily pregnant Grete to Batavia and now she was amongst friends in the camp. Her baby was eight days old.

"There is a raid on, Paula. They are now at the end of the main street. Now they are going into the side streets in groups of ten."

"There are more soldiers coming!" called Annet.

"Behind them are natives with carts. They will need those for their loot," Bep said sarcastically.

I could hear the commotion in the street, but I wasn't too worried because I knew that my children were in good hands and what else could they take from me?

Two doctors joined us.

"It will soon be our turn," Dr Flits said with a muffled voice. "There are men amongst them."

"It's been my life-long ambition to take a trip to Japan," quipped the intern, Dr Flobert.

"I would have selected a better time for that, Flobert."

"Flits, you have no imagination. I've often told you that. Don't you understand that this way the Jap will be paying for my trip?"

"There are the men, Paula. Do you recognise anybody?"

I tried to sit up to see who was walking, manacled, among the soldiers.

"Oh, I see Granddad Maaskant. I don't know anybody else. Why do they have to take a man as old as he is?"

"There will be a lot of sorrow in the camp tonight," Annet said compassionately.

"Grete can't take any more," I heard someone say, but it was already too late. Grete had opened the door, dressed in her pyjamas. Ten guns were pointed at her. In a loud voice Grete yelled "Murderers, thieves! God will punish you all!"

Dr Flits pulled Grete indoors and carefully closed the door. He put her back to bed and gave her a sedative. After a few minutes Dr Flits returned, carrying a white bundle in his arms, and stopped by Grete's bed.

"This, dear Mrs Grete, is your future." A happy smile appeared on Grete's face and she took her son from Dr Flits, fell back into the pillows and seemed to have forgotten the nasty episode.

Faking a cheerfulness he did not feel, he smiled and left the ward. When he was out of sight I heard him loudly blow his nose.

Exactly at ten o'clock the following morning the operation was done and I finally got rid of those pesky tonsils.

A few days later Dr Flits approached my bed and said "Shall we interrupt that starvation cure of yours?" He called to a nurse.

"Dinner for Mrs Paula, please, nurse; two rusks with cheese and a cup of tea."

"Well, are you enjoying that?"

"And how, doctor! It's a meal fit for a queen."

"Tomorrow you'll have one fit for an emperor and afterwards you can go home. But take care; don't talk too much and no singing for half a year."

Then he went, that little doctor with his miracle hands. But he should not have forbidden me to sing.

Once at home, I held out for three whole days, but when the moon became full and round and was shining so seductively, I picked up my lute. Francine warned me and wanted to take the lute from me.

"Don't," she said like a fussy mum.

She was too late. I was singing to my little boys "*Schlaf, mein Prinschen, schlaf ein...*"[32]

I think that I have never sung it so beautifully, with such a pure and clear voice as that evening in Batavia in Tjideng.

It did not take long for the effects to manifest themselves: I really was not able to sing a note for the following six months.

Pancakes

Nikki came with a message.

"Mummy says we are having pancakes, at 12 o'clock."

He had gone before we could ask who was invited. We chanced it for the five of us and at exactly twelve we arrived at Lies' house. We were already enjoying the smell of freshly baked pancakes as we walked up the street.

"Hello Lies. Are you trying to spoil us?"

"Certainly, come inside. The children are ready and waiting."

32 ' Sleep, my little prince, sleep.' German cradlesong by Friedrich Wilhelm Gotter in 1795, set to music by Bernhard Flies, Berlin 1796.

As quiet as mice they were sitting at the laid table holding their forks in their hands, ready for the attack.

"It's amazing that you still have the ingredients for pancakes, Lies," said Francine.

"Let me tell you about it. I had been saving a bottle of oil and a bag of flour up to now. But for pancakes you also need eggs and those…." She waited a while to increase the tension.

"I found them while I was walking near the escarpment. There is a hole in the *gedèk* (bamboo matting covering the barbed wire). Each day, a chicken came through the hole and laid an egg on our side of the fence. Nikki found the first egg. For the following four days, we walked there and found an egg each day. After that we never saw or heard that chicken again. What do you think of that?"

"It's a miracle, Lies. Maybe somebody somewhere is helping. We must never give up!"

"I thought that, to cheer us up after that *razzia* (house search) the other day, we had better do something special. That's why you are getting this festive meal."

"Thank you, Lies. We will enjoy it," we said.

When we had finished the lovely meal the children went to play outside.

"Hey! Say thank you to Lies!" Francine yelled.

The children returned and said a nice 'thank you'. Olafje, who was by now a year older than the last time Lies saw him, pulled Lies' skirt, wanting to give her a kiss. Lies lifted him up and cuddled him.

"You were so small, when I saw you for the first time, and look how Olafje has grown."

"Would you like some coffee?" Lies continued. "I don't have any real stuff, only *keddeléh*[33] substitute."

---

33 A kind of bean, used to make substitute coffee.

We gladly accepted, at the same time aware of how we were slowly getting used to having less, both in terms of quantity and quality. Each morning between 8 and 10 o'clock, *The Gate* was opened to native tradesmen to allow them to sell provisions, usually substitute food, such as the *keddeléh* coffee.

"I was thinking about that time when you were standing at my door with Olaf as a baby. I can tell you now, Paula, when Jaap arrived home and heard that I had given you shelter, he nearly beat me to death. Nikki started to scream and someone knocked on the door. That saved my life. It's probably wrong for me to say so, but I hope that Jaap will never come back."

For a moment there was an awkward silence. I looked at Francine and detected a slight irritation.

"How can you say something like that, Lies?" Francine commented.

"That is a great sin. He is your husband! But yes, I do understand somehow. In my case, I am unable to live if Willem isn't with me."

"Lies, I am so sorry you have had such an awful experience," I added.

"However, in times like these it is very difficult to stay reasonable. Most people find it difficult to keep their emotions in check. Maybe it's better not to think and talk too much about 'after the war'. We still have to get to the finishing line. 'After the war' is that light at the end of a tunnel. I never visualise anything personal, I see it more as a light for humanity, for the whole world. But before we get to that light, we must try and survive. I don't want to die here. Francine, think about our vow. Don't let your soul harden."

"Paula, that's easy to say, but I cannot think like that. I just want to have a normal life, with a husband and children. How long do we have to go on like this? We are getting old before our time."

"Francine, why long for something that can't happen yet? Besides, at this moment it depends on what we are doing with our own lives, each one of us. Life is a gift, which you need to respect and cherish. You have to keep going and function, for yourself, for your children and for your camp mates. Francine, nobody is preventing you from loving your Willem. The more love the better, especially for Willem."

I was aware of her emotions, but continued: "Take a good look around. You can praise nature for her wisdom. Fewer women are menstruating, partially owing to the lack of food, partially because of the lack of male company. I think that is good, because hygienically we are barely able to cope: we have to economise with water, there is hardly any soap, and only a lump of salt once a month.

Lies, you haven't said much. What do you think about all this?"

"Yes, I can understand. Live, but don't vegetate; use your common sense, but remain sensitive."

Francine smiled again and said "You know what I find a real nuisance sometimes?"

"No? Out with it."

"I find it a nuisance to be both the devotional Mary and the practical Martha at the same time."

"That's a woman's task. Isn't that fantastic?"

Autumn in Holland – 1995

My thoughts wander from Ampasiet and I am conscious again of my current surroundings. Writing down these memories makes me ill, yet heals me at the same time. Do not cry, it is only the past that has gone. The sun shines gold, pure gold, October gold. The leaves, green, half-yellowed, brown or even bright orange, aren't tired yet. There is still time before the November storms arrive, with their mists and rain. Then there will be time enough for the leaves to fall to the ground. Birches let their leaves flutter down with a little sigh. They are the first to fall, just as they are the first to greet me with their delicious greenery in spring each year.

Spring: won't I be too tired then, will I still be alive? When will my "*letzter Frühling*" (last Spring) announce itself? Whenever I hear Grieg or Mahler I have to cry, because the music tears my soul apart. Crying is something that you do in private, when you are sure that no one is at your front door. It is not something that you want the world to witness, you don't want people laughing at you.

"Come on, at your age you don't cry like a teenager any more."

Even if they don't say it you can see them thinking it.

When I still used to give singing lessons – what a wonderful time that was – I used to advise my pupils that, whenever their emotions would overwhelm them, they should first listen to romantic or sad music about unrequited love, such as that by Schubert and Brahms, and then let their tears flow freely.

"Then, when you have finished crying, only then listen to your dance music, which wraps all your problems, sorrows and feelings of being misunderstood in musical notes and throws it away into the air. Dance along, sing along and your soul will be liberated."

My body is becoming very old. Oh well, that is life, just as in nature. But your spirit need not age. Keep that fantastic rascal busy and it will shine and radiate. You will be able to cope with anything, conquer all misery. You can learn.

What I had written in German I had given to Padre Hamel and friends to read and they told me: "Translate it into our language. Do it now! Don't waste any time, put it down on paper. Who knows what you can still do, when this task is finished."

I let the Dutch language become part of me like a hand wriggles into a glove, first the whole hand and then one finger at a time, smoothing down the creases to make it fit perfectly.

But I must go back to my life at Ampasiet A 15 in Camp Tjideng. We were singing there too.

The piano

Each day we would drink a cup of tea beneath the shadow of the Japanese cherry tree, sitting at the table and chairs that Francine and I had moved out of the house a long time ago. Everybody was welcome at our homely tea-time gathering. Aunt Bertha and Mrs Baron, who had given us a packet of English tea on the day she arrived, also came along for a little while, but would always go for a walk after tea.

Mrs Landman, a tiny, dark-haired woman with an ivory complexion, loved to talk about art and special songs. She once gave me an album of classical songs by composers including Schubert, Schumann, Brahms, Mendelssohn, and many others. To me that was a very rare gift. Unfortunately we did not possess a piano. "But who knows, maybe one of these days we will find one thrown out in a garden somewhere," said Mrs Landman, as she handed me the album.

Every time Mrs Landman paid me a visit, she would come with her stereotypical announcement that, once again, she had to stand up for me regarding my origins. This time I spoke to her.

"Mrs Landman, just bring that lady along and she can tell me in person what she does not like about me."

"She will never do that," my guest answered.

"Never mind. She only has herself to blame with her stupid criticisms. Let's talk about something else."

Suddenly Joop and Nel entered the house calling: "Paula, there is a piano in one of the houses. If you still want it we will go and collect it before it is burnt. But where are we going to put it?"

"On the back verandah."

A few hours later a flat cart appeared in the street and ten women were dragging a heavy piano across the little bridge, through the garden and via the tiled path to its appointed place on the back verandah.

"How did you manage that?"

"We just borrowed a cart at *The Gate* and these ladies thought this so much fun that they enthusiastically offered their help."

I thanked them profusely and said, jokingly: "Send me the bill after the war."

Someone stood next to me and suggested: "The biggest job is yours. Have you had a look inside yet?" She laughed, shook my hand and said goodbye.

Suddenly everybody had left and I was by myself. Francine

had taken the children, so I had time to examine the innards of our acquisition. How happy Aunt Bertha would be.

I lifted the top lid but could not see enough, so I needed to remove the front as well. I managed quite well despite its completely rusted hinges. It turned out to be a very ancient piano, perhaps from the previous century. I hit an ivory key: no sound. The reason was that the mechanism that makes the hammer hit a string was worn. It consisted of a narrow strip of silk, which had served as food or at least dessert for some hungry rats or mice. What could I do about it? I am no piano expert and am not very technically inclined either. Wait, let's have a rummage through my sewing box. And yes, I found some embroidery silk with which I could replace the strips. After all, during a war you had to be very inventive. I started my repairs and was surprisingly successful. It would be less pleasant clearing out all those mouse droppings, which could ultimately affect the sound.

When everybody had returned home they gathered around me, full of curiosity. They had lots of comments, which I thought were rather funny, but it did not stop me from continuing my repairs.

"Oh, this is totally worn. What have you started? Have we really been giving ourselves a hernia dragging this old monster over here?"

"Leave Paula be, she will fix it."

Francine said: "I will clear up the mouse droppings together with Mengsje and Jantje. I am sure they think that'll be fun."

Aunt Bertha and Mrs Baron arrived from their walk and were happily surprised. Aunt Bertha said "When this job is done I will help you with the tuning."

"Tuning? I don't have a tuning fork."

"We'll think of something."

"What do you think? Would a pair of pliers do? I have those."

After ten days, *Chopin*, as we called the piano, was ready for use. Aunt Bertha played something.

"As a war-built instrument it will do. Perhaps we should open our ears only half-way?"

There stood *Chopin*, polished and rubbed as much as possible. We covered the damp patches with a tea towel. We felt rich and were bursting with pride.

We had announced our first concert. Mrs Baron sat in the garden together with other people. She resolved to applaud and call 'encore, encore'. The others said nothing and looked a trifle sceptical. For the introduction, Aunt Bertha played an intermezzo by Chopin and another piece by Mozart. I sang a few Schubert songs from Mrs Landman's album.

"The last number will be a boogie-woogie," Aunt Bertha said. "Everybody may have a twirl." Women and children were standing in the street, clapping to the rhythm of the music.

Then, as so often happened, a Japanese soldier came along on a bike.

"What's going on here?"

"We are singing and dancing and having fun."

The soldier laughed and said "Please stop in about ten minutes."

At least he was a cheerful Jap.

Not long after this first concert, it was Aunt Bertha's birthday. In general we no longer celebrated birthdays. We no longer even thought about them. But now we had been invited to her birthday party, so had to make an effort to make the place look a little festive. The table on the back verandah had been laid. On it stood a vase with some greenery from the Japanese cherry tree and a lit candle. Cups and mugs were ready. But we no longer had anything to offer.

Fortunately, Mrs Baron brought along a packet of delicious English tea and a packet of biscuits.

"That's the last one, I'm afraid," she said.

Relaxed, we sat around the table. The tea was ready and everyone had a biscuit in front of them. The children had been given biscuits too and were playing a little in the garden.

In the meantime Christine had also popped round to congratulate Aunt Bertha. Her eyes were no longer laughing and she no longer bothered with the children, but she had some news to tell.

"Christine, how are things with 'those down there'?" asked Francine.

"Herma has had a baby. No doubt it is a bastard."

"A child is a child, Christine, be it white, black or yellow. Every baby is lovely. You aren't jealous by any chance?" Francine teased.

"You are right, of course. Herma has had a lot of problems. She was openly called a Jap whore. But when the baby arrived she received a lot of visitors, even Mrs van Voorst. Everybody came with little clothes or other presents."

"Has the father been to visit?"

"No, but I have heard that, when it was known that Herma was pregnant, he was transferred."

"Another war baby growing up fatherless. That child will encounter a lot of difficulties later in Holland if it looks a lot like its father," I said.

"Are you coping, Christine? You are looking very tired."

"Ah, I just don't have the energy to do anything anymore."

"Be careful, hold on, will you. The Jap has to go under, not us. Do come round more often for a chat."

148

She laughed her old laugh again and promised to come.

Mrs Baron stood up and tapped a mug with a spoon, indicating she wished to give a speech. "On the birthday of this '*vuile lel*' (dirty slut) – for whom we have invited all these '*loeders*' (bitches) – I would like...."

She did not have to continue, we were in stitches. For the first time I saw Mrs Baron smile broadly.

"That's one way to teach someone a foreign language, huh, Aunt Bertha?"

I still have to laugh, thinking about it. Fortunately no soldiers were around to spoil our party.

When the war had ended and everybody tried to pick up their lives again, Mrs Baron was the only one who came up to me, embraced me, and gave me Shakespeare's collected plays bound in leather. It was a very moving and lovely gesture.

Sonei

Ode to Slamper

In April 1944 a new camp commander arrived: Sonei. He looked impeccable, a handsome man who reminded me somehow of the Nazi officer in Pomerania who had been so reluctant for me to leave the school where I worked.

Someone in Sonei's office must have been telling tales, for immediately the rumour went round that Sonei was moonstruck. We listened to the tales but did not pay much attention. We were soon to find out physically what this meant.

I will have to leave Ampasiet A in the East Indies for a moment and tell you about our dog Slamper. In 1950 we were living in a repatriation camp in Nijmegen, in so-called Nissen huts, which were barracks with wooden walls and roofs made from sheets of corrugated iron. The straw mattresses on which we slept were initially 'mountains' that needed to be flattened. That was a lovely task for the boys. Food was handed out from the communal kitchen. The camp administrator was a proper little potentate. Kindness was unheard of and, from outside the wire fence, Dutch people laughed at us or looked at us with contempt, calling out "White *baboes*".

It was blatantly obvious to us that they regarded us as pariahs, or as the Dutch called us *'opvreters, uitzuigers'* (spongers, parasites). But we pretended not to care and did not get involved with politics.

"When we are allocated a house we will have a dog."

That was a promise, which was easily made but difficult to fulfill. The children fantasised daily about what kind of dog we would share our lives with. The boys mentioned all the breeds of dogs they had come across in their books or knew from the area, such as Louis the dachshund, or Pimmy the milkman's dog. The boys preferred a big, strong dog. I was thinking more along the lines of an intelligent shepherd dog. That dog! Jantje was obsessed with it. A few times he would come home with a scruffy, emaciated stray and would say triumphantly: "Mum, I am sure he will grow into a shepherd." The snag was that a house was still a distant dream.

Finally, after nearly four years, of which two were spent in a guesthouse in the village of Lunteren, we were allocated a house in Ede. The boys still attended school in Lunteren and after school roamed around in the nearby woods. One day, they came home full of excitement, stumbling over their words.

"Mum, we have found a dog. He is so beautiful, mum, and he costs only twenty-five guilders!"

"Then we will go and take a look."

That same afternoon we rode our bikes to Lunteren. My sons took me to a house in the middle of the woods that apparently belonged to a hunter who, besides his job, also bred hunting dogs. We were greeted by a lot of barking. In the yard four puppies were playing and romping about, whilst their mother dozed in the sun. Her eyes followed her offspring and also watched the visitors. The hunter's wife gave us a friendly welcome and smiled when she saw the boys.

"I see you have brought your parents along. Come and have a look at the pups we have left. You must pay attention, for a dog chooses his own master, so you have no say in the matter," she said, laughing.

The puppies jumped up at us, sniffed at everyone and ran back to their mother. She stood up, stretched, yawned and looked at us triumphantly as if to say 'Haven't I got lovely children?' She was a fine example of her breed as well: she had long, chocolate-brown hair, a white chest and a beautiful, wagging tail with a white tip. The lady explained that the breed was a longhaired German Pointer. The mother, called Sarah, had interesting eyes, also a mark of their breed: yellow-brown with small lighter flecks, an unsentimental and self-assured look, showing an almost human intelligence; a treasure of a hunting dog.

We all sat down on the ground and waited to see what the puppies would do. They ran around us and then one of them, the biggest and the most beautiful one, came to sit on my lap. The lady said: "He has chosen you. You will be getting a gem of a dog, one in a thousand. Congratulations! May you make each other happy. The price is as I told your sons. My husband and I will be visiting you some time soon."

Our lovely new member of the family still needed a name. That took a lot of head scratching. Suddenly Jan called out: "Mum, I know a name. Slamper!"

Little Slamper became big Slamper. The vet often said 'What an enormous dog. What a happy dog.' And that is exactly

152

what he was: his eyes were filled with love for everyone in our family. He had a good life. To us he was the most beautiful dog in the world.

But Slamper was getting old. Suddenly, after having been healthy all his life, he contracted kidney and bladder problems coupled with a high fever. Despite all this he wanted to go on living as he had always done. I consulted the vet about what we should do. He did what he could, but the illness was incurable. Each morning, the kitchen floor beneath the raised dog bed was awash with urine. I was thinking about having him put to sleep. It would be no problem to call the vet at any time to come and give him the injection, once I had made up my mind that this situation could not continue any longer, especially as I also had a busy practice at home as a music teacher. But Slamper sensed this.

It was a Thursday morning when I picked up the telephone to call the vet. Slamper would not let me out of his sight. With pleading eyes he shuffled after me. The vet arrived, examined him once more and said: "I think he has had enough."

He walked towards his car to get his bag. Slamper raised himself up and his frightened eyes followed every move the vet was making. When the vet wanted to inject him, Slamper started to growl and bit him on the hand. Crying, I asked the vet to give Slamper an ordinary (non-lethal) injection, which he did. Slamper allowed that. However, the following Thursday I was determined, with a heavy heart, to put an end to the miserable situation. Slamper was following me again, it was just awful. That's when I decided to talk to him. I sat on the floor, holding his dear faithful head in my lap.

"Slamper," I started to say. "You are so ill that you are no longer able to enjoy your life. You are such a lovely dog and we love you so very much! Also think what a lovely life you have had. The doctor will not hurt you. Only your heart and ours will hurt. We will never forget you. Just let go, my dear dog. I kissed him on his head. Slamper had understood. He licked my hand and cheek, got up and walked into the kitchen to lie down on his blanket. When the vet arrived I sat down by Slamper and let the vet perform his sad duty. Slamper fell asleep for good with his head in my lap. We buried him in the garden. In our hearts and thoughts we raised a monument to him. He was just two months short of fifteen.

The Boys' House

I return to Ampasiet A 15. What I will be writing now I have told friends many times and their eyes would fill with tears.

The Japanese had become obsessed with making room for more prisoners. Our numbers had already swollen to over 5,000 people in just a relatively small area in Batavia, so everything that took up precious space would have to be taken away or even destroyed.

That morning, a bank of grey clouds prevented the sun's rays from touching our small piece of this earth. There was no beautiful tropical morning and the noises – someone shouting, the barking of a dog – sounded heavy and unfriendly. I walked to the garden gate and saw the vet cycling past.

"What's going on, doctor?" I asked.

"The dogs!" he shouted back as he disappeared around the corner.

At the same time, Elli, red-faced and clutching a white handkerchief, was walking through Ampasiet D, where Lies Matter and Christine lived.

Elli was a German woman who had followed her Dutch husband from her beautiful home town of Thüringen. She was fairly round in shape, which made her look smaller than she really was. Elli did not have any children. Together with Herma, she lived at the far end of Ampasiet D.

I got to know her at one of my monthly musical evenings, held during a full moon. Elli had been trained in an opera company. Her blue eyes, that appeared bigger through the thick lenses of her glasses, looked *"schwärmerisch, liebedürftig"* (dewey eyed, needing love) into this world. Her favourite song was *"Still wie die Nacht und tief wie das Meer soll deine Liebe sein."*[34]

Today, however, Elli was not thinking about singing. Her eyes were red from crying and tears were streaming down her cheeks.

"Elli, whatever is the matter and why are you crying?"

"Oh Paula. My Loeki, my poor Loeki!"

"What has happened to your Loeki, Elli? Is he dead?"

"Don't you know what is happening at The Gate? Loeki is the only thing I have left," Elli cried.

I took her in my arms, trying to comfort her.

"Now, tell me what is going on."

"We have to take our dogs to *The Gate*. They are all going to be killed. The vet has been giving injections to as many dogs as possible, if their owners had asked him to do so. Will you come with me?"

---

34 'Your love will be as quiet as the night and as deep as the sea.' This is possibly a quote from a classical aria, but almost impossible to track down.

"Yes, but I won't take the children."

Francine offered to keep the children at home with her and said "You go with Elli, Paula."

The closer we came to *The Gate*, the more barking we could hear. I had no idea that there were still so many pets around. People were crowding the area. Nearby stood a lorry loaded with dogs, barking and biting one another. It was a terrible sight. Then another three small, yapping dogs were thrown amidst the rest. The lorry left. Someone said: "They are being taken to the gasworks to be gassed."

In the large front garden of an empty house lay several larger dogs, carefully tied up. I looked at the animals. Their otherwise lovely eyes looked sad and dark with fear. Now and then I could hear growling and deep sighs. Japanese soldiers were inside the house, debating. In the garden we saw a pile of wooden cudgels. Then the Japanese came out, armed and yelling that boys aged fourteen to eighteen should form a line. A soldier then handed out cudgels. It was now obvious what was going to happen. A murmur went through the crowd. A soldier was ordered to fire a volley in the air. Then a harsh command, loud and clear: the boys were to use the cudgels to beat the dogs in the garden to death. A sense of horror gripped us. Then, a second volley was fired into the air. The boys, standing with legs wide apart, did not move, leaning nonchalantly on their wooden murder weapons.

The soldiers yelled at them even louder, pointing their bayonets at the boys, but even this failed to spark a reaction. Three smaller boys became so frightened that they began to lift their cudgels, but the bigger boys knocked them out of their hands. The Japs went back inside for more deliberation. We heard a lorry approaching. All the Japanese soldiers present picked up the cudgels. Cries of 'Oh God, they are going to kill our boys!' rippled through the crowd. We had been watching our boys with pride, saying 'What heroes!'

Our heroes were beaten terribly with the weapons with which they had been ordered to kill the dogs and then chased into the empty house, whose windows and doors were being battened down with criss-cross planking. That punishment in itself was already so psychologically devilish, infamous and vile. On top of that, the boys' wounds would be left untended for three whole days. They were not allowed to wash and weren't given anything to eat. After three days they were to be handed back to their mothers. From that time the house was called 'The Boys' House'.

From the watchtowers could be heard the sounds of Japanese music and singing, and there was a gorgeous smell of delicious food.

That evening, after the drama of our young heroes, there was no communal singing on my front verandah, despite the beautiful full moon. When darkness finally fell, it was a blessing. The insects started up their nightly concert. Moths were bumping around the lamp on our front verandah. The moon was like a big, red ball on the horizon. Francine was knitting a jumper for Mengsje and I tried to work on a doll, but my heart was not in it. We were silent.

The children could not sleep. Olaf said something to his older brother that only Jantje could understand. Mengsje was humming a song without words. Perhaps the children sensed the sad atmosphere hanging over us.

"I hope their little souls won't be damaged by this terrible camp period."

Jantje suddenly called out.

"Mummy, I can't sleep!"

Mengsje called, "Auntie Paula, please sing."

Jantje joined in and Olafje, who still could not pronounce the letter "s", called "Mummy, "ing!"

It sounded like a command, so I took my lute and sang a Welsh lullaby.

Sleep my baby on my bosom
Warm and cosy will it prove
Round the mother's arms are folding
In her heart a mother's love
There shall no one come to harm thee
Nought shall ever break thy rest
Sleep my darling babe in quiet
Sleep on mother's gentle breast
Sleep serenely, baby, slumber
Lovely baby, gently sleep
Tell me wherefore art thou smiling
Smiling sweetly in thy sleep?
Do the angels smile in heaven
When thy happy smile they see?
Dost thou on them smile while slumb'ring
On my bosom, peacefully?[35]

While I was singing the lullaby, some of our friends came quietly and found themselves a place on the verandah. They

35 A traditional Welsh tune which first appeared in print circa 1800. A well-known version is by the folk scholar Robert Bryan. See also: http://www.contemplator.com/wales/lullaby.html

158

came to have a quiet little chat and to give each other some comfort. The first person I noticed was Elli. She had calmed down and was luckily able to smile a little. Lies Matter, whom I saw regularly, was there too. She had once confided in me that she hated crowds.

"I feel so superfluous," she had said.

I also saw Mrs Landman, and the last one to come was Marie. She looked at me quietly with such a sad expression in her otherwise beaming blue eyes, that I had to hug her. I knew that her fourteen-year-old son Martin was also lying wounded in the Boys' House. I tried to comfort her. "Marie, it is just three days. It will be over soon."

"The nights are so long, Paula," she said, trying to be brave.

But nobody could help. We all felt a dull impotence within our hearts.

When we first came to live in Ampasiet A, Marie was living next door together with her husband Jan, her daughter Katie and son Martin. We had hit it off immediately and became good neighbours. Marie was a cheerful, lovely, plump woman with curly brown hair, and an infectious laugh. Katie was the spitting image of her mother and of similar temperament, and when those two were laughing, their noses would disappear between two rosy-red cheeks and their eyes would twinkle like candles on a Christmas tree. Jan, Marie's husband, had personally handed the keys of his margarine factory over to the Japanese commander as soon as Nippon had set foot on shore in Batavia. Had he thought this deed would gain him some advantage, or keep him from being imprisoned? As it turned out, he was one of the first civilian men to be interned.

Marie had moved house together with her children, but had

eventually become a camp internee after all. She occupied two small rooms in a large house. We didn't see each other very often. In the end the houses had become so crowded that people just relied on their housemates' company, and took an aversion to the continuous flow of new, desperate, discontented faces.

We continued talking softly, as the children had finally fallen asleep, and slowly fell silent, only to be broken a few minutes later by Francine.

"Didn't we hear before about Sonei being moonstruck?'"

"Yes, that's true. We now know that the full moon can have a bad influence on some people," said Mrs Landman.

Elli flared up.

"That's not the fault of that beautiful, celestial body! A person who can do such awful things is truly evil. Sonei can't sleep because of that moonlight and, having this position of power over us, he dreams up all sorts of ways of terrorising us."

"Yes, but in Staphorst, the village where I was born, I heard many stories about people who are moonstruck. People would walk over the rooftops in a kind of trance," said Francine.

Elli interrupted.

"That has happened in Thüringen too. You mustn't call out to them and wake them, because otherwise they might fall."

"This has all happened before. My younger sister was a bit like that. My mother would place a soaking floor-cloth on the floor next to her bed. And you know, my sister just stepped right over it," Mrs Landman told us with a smile, and continued: "It is just the gravity of the moon that influences us and all other creatures on earth. It is a natural phenomenon."

Two Japanese soldiers passed by our house, slowed down a little and then continued on their way. Maybe they were surprised we were not singing. Every now and again a soft tropical breeze would carry sounds of music towards us: Japanese music. Did they have any reason to sing? Did they feel some victorious ecstasy after that terribly cruel humiliation?

Our visitors left quietly. Francine turned off the light and we sat a while longer in silence, each of us left with our own thoughts.

A pall hung over the camp. Normally, we would hear laughter or chatter floating in the air in the evenings. But tonight, the little gas lights in the houses had been extinguished earlier than usual.

I sang to myself the third verse of "*Der Mond ist aufgegangen.*"[36]

> *So legt euch denn, ihr Brüder*
> *In Gottes Namen nieder;*
> *Kalt ist der Abendhauch.*
> *Verschon uns, Gott, mit Strafen*
> *Und lass uns ruhig schlafen,*
> *Und unsern kranken Nachbar auch.*[37]

I listened to the tropical sounds of the night: a bird flapping its wings, a *tjitjak* (a small lizard) on the wall calling its own name looking for male company. According to native belief, a *tjitjak* brings luck to a house. The Javanese *adat* (custom) says that if a young married couple moves into a house where there is

---

36 The moon has risen.
37 'Thus lay down your brother in God's name, the evening mist wafts cold, spare us, God, the punishments, and let us sleep in peace, and our sick neighbours too.' From the German lullaby 'Der Mond is aufgegangen'(The moon has come up), written by Matthias Claudius (1740-1815) and music by Johan Abraham Peter Schulz (1747-1800).

no *tjitjak* loudly calling '*tji-tjak*', it will bring bad luck. When such a small, beige coloured lizard deftly negotiates the whitewashed walls, holding on with the small sticky suction caps on its tiny feet, a young couple would be assured of happiness. Should the house still be without such a bearer of luck, the couple's friends would purposely bring a couple. Now and then one of the little creatures would, after mating, fall with a plop onto the floor – or sometimes on your neck. Many other insects were noisily busy, and there was also some animal that, screaming in fright, rushed up a tree, possibly pursued by a larger animal.

Quietly we went to bed. Our housemates wished us a good night for they could not sleep either. Mrs Fronté was crying quietly for her André, who was also lying wounded in the Boys' House. I stood for a moment next to her bed and laid a cool hand on her forehead, without saying a word. I just wanted to let her know that in our house no one was alone.

Sonei

The camp commander was moonstruck. We already knew that, and we also had already experienced what evil traits awakened in Sonei's soul when our beautiful moon was shining so peacefully in the night sky. Of course he would not go off sleepwalking. No, he left that to us. We would be called out in the middle of the night to attend roll-call in the main street, and this was occurring ever more frequently during the last months in the camp. Sleep drunk, we shuffled outside with our children to the *kumpulan*. I am talking only about our own Ampasiet quarter, for by now there were some ten thousand women and children in Tjideng camp and it would have been impossible for all of them to attend roll call all at the same time. So, the commander took full advantage of the nights when there was a full moon and each quarter would get its turn. Even the smallest children had to be present. We would quickly grab a small blanket that would give some protection on the street, so the children could lie down and sleep. This was always risky, for sleeping outside in the tropics without a *klamboe*, (mosquito net) amongst the mosquitoes and other flying insects increased the chance of contracting malaria. It sometimes took two hours before the Japs had finished counting us. Whether Sonei sometimes took pity or felt guilty, who knows, but he would promise us a delicious meal of rice and roast pork. Some lucky devils did indeed get some. So it was no lie, but there was never enough for all of us and we just felt cheated.

One night we were ordered outside again by shouts and banging on our doors. There we stood again, cold because of malnutrition. The ritual began: counting and re-counting. One person was missing. Sonei, furious, started pacing to and fro. A woman who was a doctor, took a step forward.

"It is one of my patients. I did not think it right to bring her along. She has a very high fever and is still only a child."

Her initiative cost her a horrendous beating. We were terrified.

Clenching my fists I muttered: "I'll strangle him."

People around me whispered "Don't be a fool," and pointed at my children. Later we heard that he had thrown petrol over the food, that delicious rice meal which had been promised as compensation.

It was a few days before Christmas, 1944. Boys aged ten and older and all the remaining men, including doctors, had been put on transport months ago. We had only one female doctor left. The grief of the mothers was deep as an abyss. Marie's boy, Martin, and André, the son of Mrs Fronté, and all those heroes who had been in the Boys' House had gone and nobody knew where they were, let alone what had happened to them.

In previous years we had brought a small tamarind tree inside the house, decorated it and lit some candles while we sang Christmas carols. The children were given small presents and some sweets we still had left. This year nobody even wanted to think about Christmas, or celebrating or carol singing!

Joop said "You will get a Christmas present from me. Just wait."

A few hours later Joop went into the bathroom to deposit two small parcels on top of the roof beams. It just so happened that I was watching her and I saw her suddenly freeze and her face turn as white as a sheet. What on earth was the matter with her? Our Joop, who always knew what to do and helped wherever she could. Joop was scared stiff.

I turned round and saw Sonei walking along the street. Everybody had already fled inside the house. Francine had taken cover, holding Mengsje and Olafje by the hands. But where was Jantje?

Sonei stopped at the neighbours' house, and noticed two little girls playing in the garden They were Sietske's and Vera's girls. Sietske was typically Friesian: fair hair, blue eyes and a slightly uncommunicative expression on her face. Vera came from Brabant, dark with laughing eyes, always cheerful and ready for a chat. Their children stood still when they saw Sonei and laughed at him.

I spotted Jantje in a tree and he had seen me too. I placed my finger on my mouth. He luckily understood. Then Sonei walked into the garden where the two little girls were still smiling at him. If only they had bowed. Oh, they were still so young and unconcerned.

Sonei entered the house and like a mad man started to yell and scream, pulled pictures from the walls, swept porcelain from tables and cupboards, upended furniture and threw water over the ruination he had created. The two women had to go to *The Gate* with him where they were forced onto their knees to ask for *ampun*, forgiveness. Vera did, but Sietske spat at him. Two soldiers arrived with long whips. With these whips Vera and Sietske were chased along the whole length of Avenue Trivelli and back again. They were then dragged home bleeding, with their clothes in shreds. Like a whisper campaign the story went from house to house. It was awfully quiet in the camp.

That evening, many of us looked up at the evening sky. The moon on the horizon was large and red, ready to make its journey around our world, past people good and bad and their conflicting characters. I came to a conclusion. The conquering frenzy of Nippon was on the wane. Hold on just a little longer, the end was in sight. But, how long is a little longer?

According to an article in *Time Magazine* of December 16, 1946, Sonei was shot after the war by a firing squad. I did not shed a single tear. Yet, the real planners were the top military. I don't think they were shot as well.

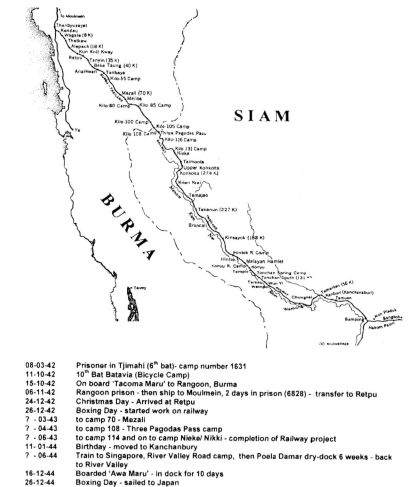

08-03-42	Prisoner in Tjimahi (6th bat)- camp number 1631
11-10-42	10th Bat Batavia (Bicycle Camp)
15-10-42	On board 'Tacoma Maru' to Rangoon, Burma
06-11-42	Rangoon prison - then ship to Moulmein, 2 days in prison (6828) - transfer to Retpu
24-12-42	Christmas Day - Arrived at Retpu
26-12-42	Boxing Day - started work on railway
? - 03-43	to camp 70 - Mezali
? - 04-43	to camp 108 - Three Pagodas Pass camp
? - 06-43	to camp 114 and on to camp Nieke/ Nikki - completion of Railway project
11-01-44	Birthday - moved to Kanchanbury
? - 06-44	Train to Singapore, River Valley Road camp, then Poela Damar dry-dock 6 weeks - back to River Valley
16-12-44	Boarded 'Awa Maru' - in dock for 10 days
26-12-44	Boxing Day - sailed to Japan
15-01-45	Arrive at Modje,via Strait of Shimonoseki;
16-01-45	start work in Motoyama coal mine (part of Fukuoka Complex)
15-08-45	Japan surrenders - end Sept transported to American base on Manila (203)

Location of the work camps along the Burma Railway and notes of Jan's
many movements during imprisonment.

Prisoners laying tracks for the Burma Railway.
(Source: *The Story of a Railway – Burma 42–45*. Watercolours by T. Inglese)

Prisoners removing boulders from the railway track.
(Source: *The Story of a Railway – Burma 42–45*. Watercolours by T. Inglese)

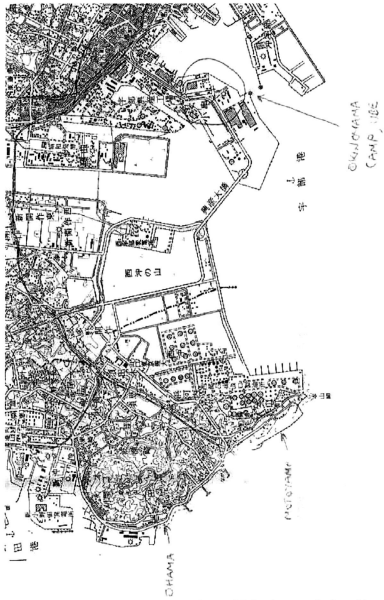

Location of the Motoyama coalmine (part of Fukuoka complex) on Honshu Island where Jan was put to work from January 1945 until the atom bombs dropped on nearby Hiroshima and Nagasaki.
(Source: Roger Mansell, Palo Alto, CA. http://www.mansell.com/
pow-resources-about.html)

Running from the atom
bomb explosion – 1945.
(Ton Hardeman 2007)

Allied Prisoners of War wave at Navy plane, 25 August 1945.
(Source US Navy Photo #80-G-490386)

Emaciated PoW at Aomari, 29-30 August 1945.
(Source US Navy Photo #80-G-490447)

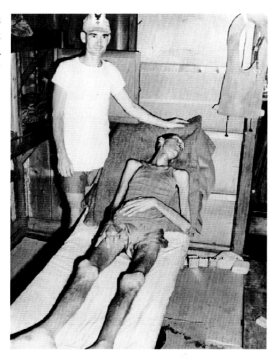

Jan (back row, third from right) and his fellow prisoners in Motoyama at the end of the war, after initial recuperation, smart in newly supplied uniforms.

Jan's Story

Hell Ship to Burma

It was now more than three years since the Japanese invaded our beautiful island and all this time we had no idea what might have happened to our husbands, fathers, sons or brothers. We had been frantic with worry in the beginning, yet now our own desperate struggle to survive at all cost and look after our children was uppermost in our minds. But, most of us who were married and had children kept a picture of our husbands, which we showed the kids every day in an effort to help them remember their fathers, in the hope they might recognise them if and when they did come back from the war. I too had a picture of Jan, and although I made sure the boys looked at it daily they were probably too young to realise who this person really was. And so it was that, when the big day eventually came, Jantje would run into the house shouting loudly that there was a strange man standing by the gate.

This great uncertainty, this not knowing about the fate of our loved ones, added immensely to our already unbearable suffering. I thought back to the last time I had seen Jan, leaving this lovely house at Ampasiet that we had just moved into, to join his field artillery unit, and then hearing of his capture and imprisonment in Tjimahi, and trying to get a pass to go and see him. It made me so sad to think that we had had so little time together in our new home, neither of us knowing we would not see each other again for such a very, very long time.

All we knew was that, as soon as our Dutch East Indies Government had capitulated on March 8, 1942, it did not take long for the Japanese to round up all military and most civilian male personnel, but from that point most of us had lost all contact with our loved ones.

I found out afterwards that, in the months leading up to the Japanese invasion, the British and Australian governments had been hastily evacuating their citizens to safer shores. For the Dutch this was impossible as the mother country had already been occupied by the Germans for two years, and was powerless. Once the Japanese had landed on Java, the Dutch East Indies authorities quite quickly lost all control, leaving many army units to their own devices to make the best of the situation.

From the prison camp in Tjimahi, where I had so desperately tried to visit him, Jan was transported back to Batavia where he joined thousands of other prisoners in the so-called *Bicycle Camp*, all waiting to hear what their fate would be. The Japanese were forever shifting their prisoners around from place to place during the war, to be put to work as slave labourers in their captured territories as well as in Japan itself. And so Jan was sent to Burma to work on the infamous Burma Railway. His ship to Rangoon was the *Tacoma Maru*, which he boarded in the harbour of Tandjong Priok, not all that far from Tjideng. This was one of the so called 'Hell Ships'.

A lot less is known about these Japanese prisoner transports by sea. Mainly old cargo ships, they lacked basic facilities and thousands of prisoners would be crammed like sardines in the holds. Jan used to tell us how, stumbling over each other in total darkness to find a toilet, the men would rarely make it in time or climb out to just relieve themselves over the railings. Jan also told us about the fate of the *romushas*, the native Asian captives, who used to be pushed into nets like animals and hung on sticks overboard. In such inhumane conditions, and in filthy excrement and stench, many prisoners would perish before they ever reached their destinations.

Rounded up for shipment in a massive hurry, the prisoners were beaten savagely if they were not boarding quickly enough. Then, for no apparent reason, the ships simply stayed in the harbour, fully loaded with prisoners, until some new instructions were given or a decision to sail was made. All the while, the prisoners would languish in the stinking, diseased and vermin ridden compartments that were slowly becoming boiling ovens, and many had died by the time the ship set sail. Journeys to Japan or wherever else the Japanese were transporting their prisoners, would often take weeks and were very treacherous, as many of the ships were torpedoed by Allied U-boats or frigates.[38] Despite marking the ships with large red crosses they were prime targets for the Allies as the Japanese always transported supplies and military materiel as well. A great majority of men were killed in this way and it is not difficult to understand why most survivors' call these ships the Japanese 'Hell Ships'.

38 Nobody should forget the story of the *Junyo Maru*, with 6,500 prisoners on board, of which 2,300 Dutch, British, American and Australian, and 4,200 Javanese. The ship was torpedoed in September 1944 by the British submarine *HMS Tradewind* with the loss of 5,620 prisoners. For more information about this disaster see: http://members.iinet.net.au/~vanderkp/junyopg1.html.

After four weeks at sea Jan reached Rangoon and on Christmas Day 1942 arrived at Retpu, his first prison camp along the Burma Railway, to start working on the railway on Boxing Day. In April 1943 Jan reached the Three Pagodas Pass camp. The Three Pagodas mark the site of an ancient battle between Thailand and Burma and now form a border between the two countries. Jan's last main work camp was camp Nieke or Nikki, where the two construction teams met, and which was apparently the site for the filming of the Bridge over The River Kwai.

Like almost all of us who had been interned by the Japanese, Jan never talked much about the horrendous sufferings in these camps, and mainly told just the funny stories. The nearby villagers were so poor themselves that they bartered food in exchange for anything and the smuggling trade was rife. So there were stories about how they would try to fool the Japanese guards when smuggling food into the camps on the way back from work on the railway, like bananas hidden under baggy pants or loin cloths. If caught, it was not so funny anymore: the smuggler would be made to eat all the bananas, and would then be thrown to the ground and guards would stamp on his full to bursting belly.

Jan helped out in the sickbays, washing the clothes of the dysentery patients, and as a result may have built up some immunity as he never caught that disease. He had a small piece of quinine tree bark, given to him by a doctor before the transports, who advised him to use it sparingly to ward off malaria attacks, although he did not escape those altogether. He later explained how his army training in the jungle had stood him in good stead for survival as he had learnt to live off the fruits of the forest. Most interesting and moving was his account of the Japanese guard in one of the camps who used to pass him an egg underneath the bamboo fence each day, and so helped save his life.

Just like music and my belief was my mainstay in Tjideng, Jan was sustained during the war by his faith, and he carried a small Bible, given to him by the head of the army training camp in Nijmegen in Holland before he left for the Far East. In this Bible he had highlighted passages that held a particular meaning for him, giving the date and the name of the camp where he was at that time.

Come unto me and all ye that labour and are heavily laden,
and I will give you rest.
Take my yoke upon you, and learn of me; for I am meek
and lowly in heart;
and ye shall find rest unto your souls.
For my yoke is easy, and my burden is light.
St Matthew 11: 28-30
Rangoon Prison, Burma December 3, 1942

On his birthday on January 11, 1944 he arrived at Kanchanaburi, which is now the site of a huge memorial and war grave. This camp was in fact very close to the stage camp Tamarkan, which is where Padre Hamel also spent a lot of his time. Who knows, they may have unknowingly met, because the Padre held regular services for the Dutch and British POWs, which meant he often saw large groups passing through from different camps on their way to other sections on the railway line. Padre Hamel gives a moving account of how one of the men passed away in his arms after a long struggle to survive. This echoes the Padre's story when he came to visit me to tell me about our friend Jo, who had died in his arms after he had given him his last rites. After the war Jan went back to visit and pay homage to his lost friends.

On hands and knees

While by June 1944 all of us in Tjideng were close to total starvation and the death toll was rising by the day, Jan was put on a railway transport back to Singapore to work in the Singapore dry docks, awaiting shipment to Japan. The Japanese had hundreds of prison camps in their own country, and many American and British soldiers had been transported directly to Japan from 1942 onwards to work as slave labourers for the large industrial concerns.

On December 6, 1944 Jan and his fellow prisoners were herded into Singapore docks to board the *Awa Maru*, but yet again the ship was kept in the docks, with the prisoners in the holds, until it finally set sail on Boxing Day 1944, marking another Christmas in conditions so inhumane that Christmas no longer meant anything at all to the prisoners.

It seems that much of our 'travels' coincided with Christmas or New Year: for both of us our first journey to the Far East was around Christmas, while Jan's major camp and sea transports all happened around that time. Christmas remained a very emotional time for the rest of our lives.

This time Jan's journey lasted three barbaric weeks, as the ship was trying to avoid allied submarines that were trying to destroy all Japanese transports. Also, by now all the waterways around Japan were heavily mined and many of the transport ships would be sailing in zig zag routes to try and avoid them, making the journeys last two or three times as long. Yet, many ships still got through, but of course the prisoners were dying daily in great numbers. I still have to weep when I think back to the story Jan told me about one such 'Hell Ship' that left Manila in the Philippines with 1,600 prisoners on board. The ship took eight long months to reach Japan in January 1945 and just 450 prisoners made it.

Jan himself used to cry when he recalled how he and his fellow prisoners, locked in the holds, could feel that their ship, the *Awa Maru*, had sailed into colder Northern waters. The ship's holds had become metal freezers, and most men, still just in their loin cloths, felt the icy metal sides stick to their bare skin, just like your tongue would get stuck to a frosty metal bar when as a kid you might playfully lick it like an ice lolly on a cold winter's day. By the time they reached Shimonoseki Strait, which separates the islands of Honshu and Kyushu, it was mid winter and the majority of prisoners had died. The ship docked at Modji where Jan and his fellow surviving prisoners went ashore. With little or no warm clothing, emaciated and diseased, they stood in the snow, waiting to be counted.

On January 16, 1945 Jan started work in the Motoyama coalmine, part of the Fukuoka complex, within the Hiroshima district and not far from Nagasaki. These were old mines that had been reopened to support the war effort, and conditions were absolutely appalling. The mine shafts were supported by pillars that were actually part of the coal seam. Jan remembered that, because the prisoners were regularly told to dig away at those supports, to increase their daily yield, many prisoners were crushed to death by collapsing pillars. The whole camp was covered in black coal dust, which turned to black mud when it snowed or rained, and there was no heating. By the end of his time in the mine, Jan could no longer walk and had to crawl on all fours to do the work, and he would not have survived for much longer.

As their chances of winning the war were rapidly receding, the Japanese became more and more violent towards their prisoners, dishing out the vilest of punishments for often irrational reasons, something we were also experiencing in Tjideng. In the mines, they were forcing the sick to work and cutting back even more on food and clothing. Jan also vividly remembered that the Japanese had the mines piped up for gas so that – if any US soldier would ever set foot on shore in Japan – they would simply turn on the gas and kill everyone. Of course, we now know that in fact the Japanese War Ministry had issued clear instructions on August 1, 1944 for the *disposition* (murder) of prisoners, PoWs, women and children internees, as well as the non-Western prisoners in the camps across their occupied and home territory, wherever and whenever an Allied invasion was expected. In fact, the plans for this so called Liquidation Plan had been drawn up back in 1942.

The Japanese had anticipated their final battle would be in September, so the horror of the atomic bomb in August that would end the hell of this war in the Far East meant that this plan was never carried out and saved millions of prisoners from execution. This shows how there are always two sides to any coin.

The Stranglehold

In low spirits

After Sonei's horrendous punishment campaigns everything changed. Nobody dared show enjoyment anymore, nor even laugh. We stayed close to the house as much as possible. Fear reigned supreme. The worst thing was being forced to watch, totally powerless, how the children increasingly suffered from starvation. They no longer played and we rarely heard their youthful laughter. It seemed to me that the typical childlike openness was slowly disappearing from their faces, and their expressions began to mirror those of adults. Banishing all these dreadful experiences from their youthful souls will require a huge effort when the time comes.

Meanwhile, our money had gone, our clothes had worn out and sewing any clothes was no longer possible as my sewing machine had been taken ages ago in a raid. I was keeping just one cotton shirt for better days. The raids were getting more and more thorough: we had to sit or stand outside by the side of the road and anything still being hidden would be found. I always kept a supply of lamps and candles, because I had a phobia about being alone in the dark. This time the lamps were in a drawer, yet they too were found. One consolation was that everything that we had to hand in was being collected and stored at *The Gate*, according to one of the people who worked there. Maybe one day I would get my *Singer* back.

During one of these unreasonable search campaigns, a Japanese soldier who spoke Dutch came and sat amongst us and said: "Ladies, don't risk being punished. Give them those things, if they demand them. After the war you have all these things again, only they will be new and better."

It was inevitable that someone should ask: "And who will give us those new, better things?"

The Japanese soldier shrugged and repeated: "Everything will change."

"When will the war be finished?" someone ventured to ask. Ouch, he found that a bit too embarrassing. The soldier or junior officer changed tack diplomatically. He smiled and covered his eyes with both hands and then his ears. See nothing, hear nothing. Then he went on his way.

Food now came from the soup kitchen and each house had received a number. Ours was number 75. A girl came round daily on her bike with details of the day's food. She sounded like a professional announcer. Sometimes I still hear her in my dreams:

"Numbers 1 to 75, come and collect rice."

That was often at eight in the morning. At twelve the announcement would be for *sayur* (a light vegetable stew) and at five for bread.

We saw how indifferent our fellow camp mates were becoming and that we no longer did things together, like cooking. Everyone had to manage their own rations, which were getting smaller each day. Most of them would eat everything all at once. I thought it would be better to stick to a routine: bread for breakfast, also bread for lunch, if there was anything left, and at six a bowl of rice with *sayur* (vegetables). Sometimes we would be given soup with a bit of meat floating in it.

Each time I tried to save a piece of bread for particular occasions, for instance after a punishment, I called that comfort bread. Olaf was three years old now and could already read the time. He just used to wander around among everyone in the house, sucking his thumb. He no longer wanted to play. He kept on coming inside to stare at the clock. Food at six o'clock. Then he would perk up a little.

What I did notice though, was that many people, including some in our house, had begun to write.

"What is it you are writing? If it is about the camp you'll have to be careful that Sonei does not get to know about it."

"Aren't you writing then?"

"What should I write about?"

"Well, recipes of lovely cakes, like cream profiteroles, all made with the substitute ingredients we are now using."

"Do you still want to eat that substitute stuff after the war? I can't imagine that," I answered.

"I have heard it is better not to get too obsessed about food. Your gastric juices will be stimulated and it will soon wear you down even more," Francine interjected.

"What are you doing then?"

"Me? I just read my books again."

"Do you still have those?"

"Feel free to borrow them!"

"No, thank you. German is far too difficult for me."

"I also have some Dutch books."

"Oh no thanks, I can't concentrate anyway."

The girl from the soup kitchen rode past on her bike

shouting the message that we could collect some *lombok*. Lombok is a paste made from red chili peppers and is rich in vitamin C, very good for the children and for us. But vitamin C was no big supplement to our meagre rations. Everybody was losing weight and most of the children were developing swollen tummies and rake-thin legs. We realised we were well on our way to serious malnutrition and the end was not even in sight. Everyone wore slippers or went barefoot, little girls wore threadbare dresses, and lots of children, as well as adults, were suffering from tropical sores. If an outsider had been able to observe us you might have heard him say: 'What a shabby lot. It's worse than a gypsy camp.'

Smuggling for food with the villagers outside the camp, by swapping old clothes or other items in exchange for food, had been rife throughout the camp years and many women risked the severest punishment and even group punishments if they were caught. This time though I heard something dreadful. Many women had become addicted to smoking and I wondered how they managed to obtain cigarettes. It had to be by smuggling. It turned out that there were mothers who exchanged their food rations and those of their children for cigarettes.

Many people also supplemented our meagre rations with slugs and snails, and my friend Christel had just caught a snail. I had not expected her here in Tjideng. She, together with a group of thirty others, of which ten were children, had been in several camps and had finally arrived in here. She laughed and asked me: "Are you feeling hungry?"

"Of course not, what on earth would give you that idea? It is *Schlaraffenland* here." (Land of Plenty).

"Well, in that case, I have a delectable dessert for you. It will do you good. I have already removed some of its slimy 'dresses' for you. You do the rest, Paula, while I will stoke up the fire. We are going to cook this creature."

I shuddered at the sight of the slippery animal.

"How many slimy 'dresses' do I still need to remove, Christel?", I called.

"Only two more!"

Half an hour later, the snail had been cooked and we ate it with great gusto. We imagined tasting exquisitely prepared liver. Despite that war success, though, we never again had snail on the menu.

During the 1960s I was still in regular contact with Christel in Amsterdam. Her Jo did not return from the war. Fortunately I was able to give her Jo's personal belongings given to me by Padre Hamel.

One day however some encouraging news did the rounds in the camp. We could collect white knitting cotton from *The Gate*, with which we had to knit socks. A pair of socks, just straightforward knitting, was worth a lump of *gula djawa* (dark Javanese sugar). Therefore, those who loved knitting had soon stockpiled sugar in their cupboard.

But that was not all. Many people said those socks were destined for dead Japanese soldiers, for they were not allowed to enter heaven with bare feet. Whether or not this was true I never fathomed. It was, however, a morale booster for many and I often heard: 'That's another Jap dead.'

It was frightening how cold we felt in the evenings, nights and early mornings, a sign of how far malnutrition progressed. The knitting ladies would be sitting on their chairs in the middle of the street, in the slowly warming sun.

184

We kept a fire burning all the time now in our garden, on which everybody could boil her kettle of water for a cup of *keddeléh* coffee. Small slivers from a long, square wooden post, left over from the original fencing, and requisitioned by Joop and Nel one day, were carefully fed to the fire. But in the end the post was getting shorter, so Joop said: "I know where to find a few more posts."

Our unique little fire would not be allowed to die.

Hygiene in a crowded house

The months of the new year (1945) inched past slowly. If months were able to while away their time as slothfully and despondently as we did, then we would make good allies. Have you ever looked at a clock and wondered how long it takes for the second hand to move? A second can be long, oh so long. I would like to write about something nice but there was only misery and hardship. It was as if a snake was watching us, ready to coil around us and strangle us. Camp Tjideng no longer contained ten thousand women and children. The number was now estimated to be between eight and nine thousand, many of whom were sick, but we were still oblivious: the great death toll was yet to come. I thought back to those first months when the camp was still open. Famous people would perform for us, after having been snatched from their tours and interned. The pianist Lilly Kraus gave a concert. Lilly would often rise up from her piano stool with a deep sigh when she played music by the composer Chopin. Little Corrie Vonk, an excellent cabaret artiste, entertained us. Later on all this had stopped. Except here at A 15, where we continued singing until nobody felt like it anymore.

And still more people were assigned to our house. Three of them, Mrs van de Berg and her two daughters, Guus and Beatrix, took the kitchen at the end of the tiled path, next to Mrs Baron. For another three, Mrs van Dijk and her two children, we had to empty a bedroom, so Joop, Nel and little Bernard moved into my bedroom. Joop borrowed a big hammer and chisel and made a large hole in the wall so that they had their own way out of the house. In fact, most walls in these old houses now had holes chopped in them to allow people to get in and out, as with all the budging up not everybody had their own entrance.

That left me, with Jantje and Olafje, but there were no more rooms available. I offered to take the half-covered back verandah. All our housemates helped me move my bed. With Mrs Fronté's permission, we placed the stained-glass windows over the other open half of the verandah and hey presto, it now looked nice and cosy. Even our *Chopin* could stay put.

When the first rains came it turned out that our arrangement was not waterproof. But not to worry: we rolled the mattress up towards the head of the bed and waited for the rain to stop, comforting ourselves with a piece of bread or a small piece of *gula djawa*. Despite everything we were still grateful to be living in the tropics, where, even in the rainy season, the sun would shine for a few hours and everything that was wet would dry quite quickly.

One morning Francine woke up and thought the roof was leaking. She called me.

"Is it our roof or is it raining? I have such a horrible taste in my mouth."

I examined her *klamboe* and spotted some damp, yellow

stains on the circular piece of cotton. Oh, how awful, rats!

"Francine, it isn't raining and the roof is not leaking. A rat has been walking over your *klamboe*. You have tasted rat's pee. Rinse your mouth out and gargle with some salty water."

It made her feel sick.

This experience highlighted the importance of hygiene in the house. Every time new people had moved in with us we would discuss with them the use of our toilet.

"*Please do not throw anything inside the toilet which may cause obstructions.*"

When Francine asked this, some would look a bit down in the mouth, but they would nod. When I asked, their eyes blazed, but they would also nod. Just imagine being told by a *Mof* what you should or shouldn't do! But they had not got to know us yet.

Following the arrival of the last seven housemates, Francine came up to me and said: "Paula, I have been thinking. What are we going to do with so many people living in this house? The soap and cleaning materials have run out and we have less and less water. Hygiene is part of surviving, so let's make a plan together. You know what happened to me yesterday."

So we put a list together of general chores and devised a roster. Then we called together all our housemates, all 21 of us.

"Dear housemates. We now have to live with 21 people in this small house. We won't be able to squeeze one more in and we don't know how long the situation will continue like this. Do you agree with Francine and me that we don't want to succumb here, but want to leave this hellish place reasonably healthy?"

"Absolutely" I heard, but there was some grumbling as well.

"How will we manage our personal hygiene and that of our

allocated living space? Francine and I have hung up a list near the toilet. Everybody can read there what we must do to keep things clean. Please do not leave food lying around. You know what has happened to Francine. So, we do not want any rats, lice or fleas, but we do want some optimism and belief in the future."

"Nice words," someone said. "But what happens if things get even worse and we have less food and water?"

"We will have to cross that bridge when we come to it. Console yourself with the knowledge that, if things get worse for us, it means Nippon is getting hit harder, and the war will be finished sooner."

There was now also too little water to clean one's whole body. The fresh and clean image of the European woman had disappeared. I possessed just two shirts and two pairs of shorts. But, I was still very proud of my hair; it always looked thick and healthy. The secret for this, which I would remember for better times, was an aloe vera plant in our garden. Its wide and thick leaves produced a lovely, gelatine-like substance when you squeezed them. This was my war shampoo.

What would haunt me for the rest of my life was the stench. Although our toilets were still working, we no longer had enough water to flush them, and they were of no use to us now. So, we were forced to use a chamber pot for our needs and empty that each day at the end of the *slokan*, Jantje's hell, with a small mug of water for rinsing, and that in the tropics! I do not think that anyone who has not experienced that kind of thing can ever imagine anything so terrible. My sense of smell has been seriously damaged. I can no longer enjoy the fragrance of roses, lilies, or even perfume.

More gruelling punishments

It is very frustrating to be punished when you have no idea what crime you have committed. So it happened that the girl on the bike was calling certain house numbers for which food could be fetched, and that was it. Those living in the houses whose numbers had not been called, were being punished. One day the whole camp was given soup. Everybody was delighted. Delicious! Warm soup, even though it was rather thin. But then we noticed that the soup gave off a very strange smell.

My memories fly back to my youth. At home we had slaughtered a pig, he had been my friend. The entrails were cleaned out for making sausages. And that was the exact smell that came off the soup in our pan. It was soup made from entrails. We were appalled. Most of us threw it in the *slokan*, but I thought it may contain some nutrition.

Jantje yelled "Mummy, no soup! It stinks of poo!"

Olaf repeated very decisively "Poo!"

"Do you want to grow up big and strong?" I asked. Yes, they said they wanted to.

"In that case, pinch your nose and open your mouth." The poo soup was eaten.

We were also often punished without ever knowing the reason. For example, some women had been told their husbands had died. Was this an administrative error or was it just to needle us? For after the war these men did return home. This was one of the psychological strategies to undermine the women and children. How afraid the occupiers actually must have been, to stoop to that level.

Encouraging distrust was another means to punish. It was

decided that from now on we had to fetch food in one go for all the inhabitants of the house, and we could borrow saucepans for this. The food then had to be doled out by only one person. What a job! As "*capalla rumah*" (head of the house) that role fell to me. This was one of those infamous tricks of the Jap, for they knew this would cause quarrels in most households.

My ladle came into action. All the women stood around me, watching me hawk-eyed to see that I was fair and did not give myself a few extra grains of rice.

"Just watch me carefully and if I don't do it right, please tell me," I said. I had forestalled any grumbling and some walked away. They had faith in me.

"Wait, I have a question. Would you agree that we give the little children a few more grains, for we would not want to leave them behind in this murky place?"

People nodded affirmatively or mumbled.

"Of course."

From then on they left me to it. We had formed a special relationship in the house, almost a family even, in these times of hardship and suffering.[39]

Later Francine said to me: "Each evening there is such a lovely smell of brown beans and bacon coming from the room of one of the families. I feel almost inclined to knock and ask them to invite us."

"If they have that much food, they would give their rations to the children, surely?"

"Ha, ha, don't make me laugh. They are far too afraid they might lose weight."

39 This sentiment has been confirmed by Beatrix van den Berg, one of the last arrivals at Ampasiet A 15, now living in Australia. She said that they had been very lucky during their various house moves and always had stayed in places where the atmosphere was positive, unlike very many other places.

I had indeed noticed how well they all looked. They never joined us for a chat. When the war had finished, they loaded up a flat cart which, besides their personal belongings, was filled with tin cans and candles, some of which started to roll from the cart into the *slokan*. They could easily have held out a while longer!

The Japs had invented other new ways with which to terrorise us. One of those had to do with our life-sustaining water. I was convinced that the water was purposely turned off either by the occupiers locally or on orders from Tokyo. Could we now be secretly triumphant? For it was becoming quite obvious that Japan would be the big loser in the end. Most of the camp inmates did not give this a thought. They had even lost all interest in socialising. They no longer cared about anything, only about water. After all, we were living in the tropics. All the taps were dry, no longer functioning. Our bare essentials of life had been cut off.

In the garden of each house was a standpipe with a tap. It only worked at night. So we had put all the tubs, buckets, pots and pans that we had in the garden ready to be filled. We took turns at filling up, each waking the next person. And, for each inhabitant, including the children, a saucepan full of water needed to be emptied into the *mandi* tub. After all, we needed to wash. And then it happened that someone stole some water because she was too lazy to wake up during the night.

Porridge

Meanwhile, the torture continued. Every week the rations from the kitchen shrank in size. We were totally malnourished. Some people were no longer able to walk because their legs were so swollen with oedema. Others could still walk but were as thin as rakes. For ten days now we had been given pans filled with a kind of porridge and a lump of bread. No rice, no *sayur*, not even soup made from entrails. The porridge had a glassy, grey appearance and was totally devoid of any taste. It looked very much like wallpaper paste. We had to eat it if we did not want to die of starvation. I could no longer swallow. Each spoonful had to be helped along with a mouthful of water. Jantje and Olafje loved the porridge though, because they received our ration as well. I think it must have been its quantity. Finally they had warm, filled stomachs.

When we were given a house in Batavia after the war had ended, the boys often asked: "Mummy, when are we going to that camp again? We loved that porridge."

I often took the children back to that dreadful place and tried to explain to them a little about what we had had to endure. But they were still too young to be able to understand.

If you wanted to, you could hire yourself out as a "corpse carrier", because the great death toll had begun. You had to carry the corpses to *The Gate* from where the victim would be handed over to someone else. We never knew to whom. It was very heavy work, and what was the pay? A lump of *gula djawa*? Nobody ever knew.

One day the 'corpse carriers' came by and I saw a body, swollen with oedema, lying wrapped in a *tikar* (bamboo mat) on a big improvised stretcher laden with bodies, the stretcher so rickety that bodies were nearly falling off. I was talking with a small group of women, when more dead were carried past us.

One stretcher was lowered to the ground for just a moment, as one of the bearers paused to wipe the perspiration from her forehead. I looked at the body on the stretcher and saw the dead face of Marie. She must have died recently for her face had not yet started to decompose. I had never seen such an expression of sorrow and misery. It pierced my heart. Marie, who, when alive, had been like a ray of sunshine to everybody surrounding her. In all those years in the camp I had not shed a single tear, but now, seeing the sorrow on her face, something inside me broke. I was no longer the one who was able to take all the blows that fate had dealt us. I was no longer that organising, comfort giving, happy, singing person I liked to be. No, for that moment I became an uncontrollably sobbing, hurt child. Once again it was Francine at my side, taking me into her arms.

"That is good. Have a good cry. No one here is laughing at you. Come, let's go to our children who are playing at Christine's."

The year 1945 was now into its fourth month. People were suffering dreadfully and asking in desperation how much longer the war would go on. The exodus of the dead had begun. Usually between twenty and twenty-five corpses were taken away daily. But we no longer saw the corpses being transported during the day. The stretcher-bearers could no longer cope, and I think the Japanese had decided to remove the bodies at night only. We did receive some Red Cross parcels which were opened under supervision, but those were like a drop on the red-hot hunger plate.

In my vivid imagination I again saw that Japanese snake with its powerful, yellow and black body and treacherous eyes wriggling closer and closer. Would it succeed in choking to death, with its asphyxiating stranglehold, those who had not yet succumbed to starvation? We had never counted the years, months and days. Christmas had always been a milestone on which we focused. But it was now a good few months since the last Christmas, which we had not celebrated, and we were longing for this to end. Some people were so desperate that they were saying: "Let the filthy Jap end it all. That would be better than letting us die slowly, like animals. Look at our children, ragged, sick little creatures, already damaged in body and soul."

Fortunately not everybody was that negative. There were enough of us left who would keep on fighting. And, there were even some women who stayed optimistic and would every now and again tell a little joke.

Marian approached me and said: "Paula, you are a good judge of the situation. What do you think, how long will this continue?"

"Let's do some calculations. After the Red Cross parcels things quickly went downhill. Less food, more punishment, more torture. I think the Jap is sorely afraid, more than we are. We do not know what is happening at sea, in the air, on the islands and even in Japan itself."

"And what if the Jap is so desperate with fear he will kill us all?"

"He has been doing that for ages now. Just look at yourself."

"I will never look into a mirror again."

"Never? Hopefully you will, later on, when we have recuperated and have once more become beautiful young women! Keep your spirit up!"

The last *kumpulan*

The *kumpulans* continued and were exhausting. Everybody had to attend, no matter how weak or ill they were. Then, one day at around ten in the morning, we were summoned for a roll call in the main square. Tired and indifferent, we shuffled through the camp, not realising or noticing how lovely the morning was, how beautifully the birds were singing, as if they were singing for the first time. Clouds as light as a feather drifted past the sun. There was something tranquil in the air, suffused with a tinge of suffering. We did not have to stand to attention in rows. What a relief, that slight relaxation of attitude.

A Japanese officer stood on a small stage so that he could oversee us all and we were forced to look up at him. Something was different, that was clear. There was no longer an aura of power emanating from him, more a loss of spirit, a feeling very familiar to the rest of us. If we had been able to, we would now have pricked up our ears like dogs do, as if to say: 'What is the matter, master? There is something different about you. Has something happened?'

Finally he started to talk. It was clear that he found it very difficult, but he pulled himself together and added a note of courage to his voice.

"Ladies, we have to tell you that Nippon has been forced to capitulate."

'Mr Nakama, what will you be saying now?' I rejoiced inside.

He went on.

"The capitulation came after a new type of bomb was dropped on my country, which has resulted into hundreds of thousands of victims. You are now free."

We stood there, a crowd of shabby looking women and children. We were poorly dressed, some in rags, malnourished, the children with swollen tummies and thin legs covered in tropical sores. The children's eyes, large and uncomprehending, looked up at the adults. When is the girl on the bicycle coming, calling out 'Numbers 1 to 75 to come and collect the rice?'

We were just as uncomprehending, looking up at that well-fed Japanese officer in his impeccable uniform standing on the stage. He looked defeated, but still in control of his emotions.

What was he talking about? A new kind of bomb had been dropped on Japan that had killed a hundred thousand people. We could not even imagine anything like this. It was too far from our 50 cm. We stayed silent. Nobody cheered, nobody moved. The officer continued.

"Ladies, listen carefully. For the time being you must stay inside the camp. We have taken it upon ourselves to be responsible for your safety. Don't try to leave the Gate. It will be dangerous for you out there."

We were too weak. His words did not touch us. But didn't he say 'peace'? He said a word for which we would not be punished. Peace, what was that? That needed a flag, didn't it? Stay in the camp: there was danger outside. Is that peace?

We shall have to wait. If only we were given more and better food. And we were: they gave us tinned fat herring in tomato sauce. It made us sick: round as barrels on legs like stilts, no longer able to fit in our clothing. Beri-beri, oedema! Don't die! We did not fight to survive, only to die now. There must be a different life around the corner.

But where and when?

This was August 1945. The terrible Second World War had ended – but nobody had a Dutch flag. And nobody celebrated the liberation.

Life slowly came towards us, to greet us with a smile.

We arrived back in Holland in 1950, and were finally allocated a house after four years of waiting in cramped barracks, overcrowded guest houses and even an unused castle.

But the flag?

Long after we were settled in, there was still no flag. The end of the war was celebrated on May 5, while for us August 15 signified the definite end of the Second World War. Well, at least each year on that day we could have a delicious "*rijsttafel*" with the sole purpose of indecently filling our bellies.

Then, on August 15, 1999, fifty-four years too late, they finally hoisted the flag on top of all the official buildings. We could no longer get excited about that. For us, to use a Dutch expression, it was "*mosterd na de maaltijd.*" – too late to be of any use. The German poet Heinrich Heine had said it once before: "*In Holland kommt alles 50 Jahre später*" – In Holland everything happens 50 years later.

Crossing

This life was heavy
Tiring and sad
This life was enriched
by art and music

Thank You for the gifts
Thank You for the work
Thank You for the beginning
Thank You for the end

I am standing before Your Gate
O, Lord of all
You called my name
Softly I am knocking

Paula Kogel

Paula with Jantje (left) and Olaf in their first new home after the camp, in early 1946. Jantje still has bandages on his tropical sores.

Jantje (left) and Olaf.

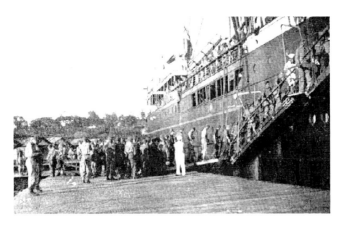

Jan was sent on recuperation leave to Holland in 1947. The family sailed on board the SS *Volendam*, seen here on the quay while troops are boarding for that journey.

Paula's parents, Germany 1947.

Paula with Jan in Tjimahi in 1948 – with the boys and baby Lore.

The house in Tjimahi as it was when Jan visited in the mid eighties.

Paula's great friend Else, here with her daughter Erica around 1946.

The MS *Amarapoora* – built in 1920 in England. Used as a hospital and troopship and to repatriate survivors. Scrapped in Osaka, Japan, in 1959. (Source: Clydesite: see www.clydesite.co.uk/clydebuilt/viewship)

Paula with the children in the repatriates camp in Nijmegen, Holland, in July 1950. Note the heavy black shoes, a Red Cross regulation issue at the transition camp en route through the Suez Canal.

Paula with Liesel (seated in pram) and Lore in the Nijmegen repatriates camp, winter 1950.

Castle *Bruinhorst* at Ederveen, the first contract guesthouse after the
Nijmegen camp.
(Source: Gemeentearchief Ede, Netherlands)

Paula with Liesel (left)
and Lore on the scooter,
Ederveen, around 1952.

Villa *Boekhorst* in Lunteren, the second and much larger contract guesthouse.
(Source: Gemeentearchief Ede, Netherlands)

Liesel (seated in pram) with Lore (pushing) and niece in Amsterdam during visit to Jan's parents – around 1950.

Paula at her piano,
with her beloved lute,
during her successful
musical career.

Christmas 1965 – Paula's first concert with her private music
practice students.

Paula and her church children's choir, the 'Lutherroosjes' in the 1960s.

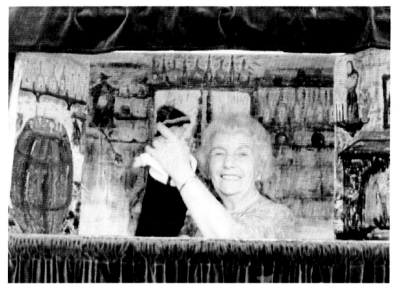

Behind the scenes of Paula's puppet theatre.

PART THREE

Rebuilding Life

Rebuilding Life

Reunions and separations

The war might have ended but freedom was as elusive as ever. Indonesian Nationalist fervour, which the Japanese had been steadily encouraging since long before the war, had reached boiling point and just two days after the Japanese surrendered, the leading Indonesian nationalists called for an independent republic. Armed Indonesian youth gangs were marauding the streets, mercilessly killing the 'Dutch' – including mixed race Eurasians and other Europeans. This early period of wild and uncontrolled murder campaigns, from liberation into 1946, was called the *Bersiap* period and marked the beginning of the war of independence, which ultimately lasted until 1949. The war itself was highlighted by two specific periods of fighting called '*Politionele Acties*' (Police Actions), or military counter insurgency campaigns.

It clearly was too dangerous for anyone to be outside the camps, and on instructions from the temporary British authorities, the former Japanese camp guards now became the women's protectors. Camp life continued, albeit in better circumstances, and many Europeans still living outside the camps or found wandering in search of their original homes or their families in other camps risked being killed by the mobs and were urged to move into the camps for their protection. My brother Jan told me how he, by then a seven-year-old boy, and Olafje, all of four years, were adventurous and eager to find out what life was like outside the camp's fences, and decided to go and wander out into the nearest *kampong*. They did not get far. They were spotted by a group of village youngsters who – screaming '*Merdeka*' (freedom) and armed with large machetes – chased them back to the camp, threatening they would chop their heads off when they got hold of them.

"As fast as our feet could carry us, we raced back into the camp for safety…,"he remembers.

Not long after, the British internees were among the very first to leave, but immediate evacuation for the Dutch women and children was impossible. Back in Europe, Holland was in total disarray and financial ruin after its years of German occupation and unable to set up an interim Dutch Government in its colony, or organise ships for immediate repatriation. Gradually, however, the men liberated from the civilian camps came to find their loved ones and repatriation gathered momentum. But most of the Dutch soldiers who had survived the prison camps were not allowed to return to be reunited with their families. Instead, they were immediately re-mobilised and forced into renewed fighting in the war of independence.

At that time, in September 1945, Lady Mountbatten, the wife of Lord Mountbatten, the last British Viceroy of India, toured the camps in Java with a photographer to record the conditions after the suffering that the women and children had endured for all those years. They found emaciated women, some with dazed minds, and children covered in tropical sores, their bellies swollen from hunger. Because medical supplies were limited at that time, many women died even though the war had ended. Other survivors died because they ate too much too quickly after such a long time of starvation. Many Tjideng internees, too weak to remain in the camp, were taken to nearby hospitals. During my extensive research I made contact with a former Dutch nurse who told me that she and five other Dutch nurses had been flown in from Australia in a B29 bomber aircraft to take care of the women from Tjideng. Her words graphically illustrate the physical and mental state of many of the women, psychologically damaged by those long years of deprivation and torture: "*I was working in a women's ward with mostly victims from camp Tjideng. Three women in beds next to each other had each managed to keep a small item hidden from the Japs. The woman in the middle was in very bad shape, and the women in the beds either side of her had started to argue over who would get what after she died. This was something we did not expect: the totally demoralised state of the victims. These victims also took it out on us, throwing mess tins at us and accusing us of eating their food. We had to introduce food in very small amounts as their bodies had to be slowly adjusted.*"

In Japan, meanwhile, the PoWs working as slave labourers in coal mines and industrial complexes, some of which were close to Hiroshima and Nagasaki, were mostly unaware that the war had ended. Rumours about atomic bombs were rife though, fuelled by prisoners saying they had heard the noise of explosions, seen flash lightning, or had even seen strange clouds on the horizon. My father's camp complex was about 40 miles away from Nagasaki, and he always said how lucky he was to have been in the mine underground when the bomb was dropped.

That we should be saved from our enemies,
and from the hand of all that hate us.
St Luke I-71
Motoyama, Japan, August 28, 1945

Although the Japanese informally surrendered on August 15, the Americans were only too aware that the Japanese would fight to the last man to defend their country if anyone set foot on the main island. This meant that the prisoners were not properly told until after the formal surrender on September 2, and had to stay inside the camps until they could be repatriated. But many of them began making their own way back home, especially the ones with families who were desperate to find out what had happened to them.

My father was among the prisoners who were too starved and sick to move and simply had to wait until the Americans finally came to rescue them, on September 15, 1945. Together with fellow survivors too weak to travel unsupported, he was transported by train to Nagasaki where he boarded the USS *Sanctuary* to Okinawa, and from there transferred to Manila in the Philippines, where he joined a large group of Dutch survivors recovering in hospitals. In November they were all taken to Indonesia by British ships, such as the *HMS Glory* or *HMS Colossus,* and ordered straight back to active army service. My father had to join his army unit in Balikpapan on the island of Borneo, the town where he and my mother were married before the war. It was not until mid February 1946, six months after his release from Japan, that he was given leave to go and see his family in Tjideng and to arrange a transfer for them out of the camp into a new home. When he arrived at the gate of the house on Ampasiet A, Jantje ran indoors shouting: "Mummy, mummy, there is a strange man at the gate." The strange man at the gate had changed considerably from the man in the picture who the boys had been told was their Daddy during all those years in the camp.

Sadly, after just three weeks he was called back to Balikpapan, only for his Artillery unit to be transferred back to Batavia eight weeks later, to fight against the nationalists. Although nearer his family, he was yet again away from home for long periods. Consequently, since the end of their imprisonment, there had been virtually no opportunity for my parents to properly recover from their ordeals or to rekindle their strained and deteriorating relationship. In June 1947 he was at last given recuperation leave and the whole family sailed to Holland on board the SS *Volendam*.

Staying with his parents in Amsterdam, my father discovered there was very little room for a family of four, and also little sympathy for their ordeal. They, like others who had been repatriated from the Far East, were reminded that "We have had the 'hunger winter' here, and people died of cold and starvation. All we had to eat were tulip bulbs. At least you were away in a warm and sunny country. Why are you complaining?"

We discovered years later that during the war many in my father's family had been very active in the Resistance, and had risked much in helping to smuggle Jewish children to safety in Switzerland. His sister Co, being dark haired and with dark-brown eyes, had made numerous trips, posing as a mother taking her children, until one day she was betrayed. Being in Switzerland at the time, she was no longer able to return home as there was now a price on her head, and she spent the rest of her life in her adopted country.

After only four months leave in Holland, the army was hot on my father's heels again, and he was ordered back for duty in the Far East. My mother and the boys went to Germany for a two-week visit to see her parents, and Jantje was especially keen to meet his uncle Gustav, my mother's favourite brother, whose name she had given Jantje for his middle name. My brother still remembers this long train journey, passing the ruins of towns and cities ravaged by bombs, and then seeing in contrast the beautiful forests in the countryside near his grandparents' home.

In May 1948 my mother, by then heavily pregnant expecting me, and the boys arrived back in Batavia on the MS *Oranje*, ending another separation of more than seven months. My father had been posted to Tjimahi, an army town in central Java, where he had first been held prisoner in the very early days of the war, and they finally seemed to be able to lead a happy family life. Unfortunately, the Independence war was still raging and by December 1948, just over four months after I was born, the second 'Police Action' (Counter Insurgency campaign) had started. My father was called up to fight and was once more repeatedly away from home for long periods. Yet again, my mother found herself alone, this time not only with the boys, but also with a little baby girl and expecting her fourth child, never knowing for sure whether her husband would return safely. These constant absences became such a strain on their relationship that my father decided to leave active service, and after completing a training course he transferred to an administrative post. Not long afterwards, in October 1949, my sister Liesel was born.

Meanwhile, Holland had come under intense pressure from the major powers, such as the USA, Britain and Australia, to end the hostilities, and after intervention by the Security Council, had reluctantly agreed to negotiate the handing over of the colony, and Sovereignty was agreed on December 27, 1949. As a matter of fact, the *Republik Indonesia* had actually been established on August 17, 1945, resulting in the protracted war of independence, and only as recently as August 2005 has the Dutch Government recognised that date as the formal date of independence.

Newly independent Indonesia immediately ordered all Dutch nationals, as well as Indonesians married to Dutch partners, to leave for destinations of their choice, but many had no option but to return to Holland, and a second repatriation was under way.

It was time for our family to leave too. My father was keen to join the Australian army and settle there, but my mother desperately wanted to go back, especially to see her own family in Germany.

As my father had been posted to the bureau of repatriation, he was now responsible for transports for all Army personnel, while many civilians had to make their own arrangements, or wait their turn, just like his own family. Eventually, he managed to book a ship for a sailing to Holland in May 1950. By then, the days of returning on big passenger ships had long gone, and the only transportation available was an old English-built coal freighter, partly converted to carry passengers: the *MS Amarapoora*. Sadly, because he was not allowed to leave until he had finalised the Army repatriation programme, my father had to stay behind in Batavia until September. So, alone my mother sailed, with us four children, to a new life in Holland. For the two boys this was their third long journey across the oceans and it is little wonder that both of them became sailors,

Jan in the Merchant Navy and Olaf in the Marines. My mother talks about this journey home in Part One, in the chapter called Suez Canal.

Settling in Holland

On arrival in Holland there were none of the official welcoming committees on the quays that had greeted the first repatriates returning in 1945 and 1946. In fact, there did not seem to be much of a welcome at all. We were allocated a 'home' in old army barracks in Nijmegen, which had been converted to a repatriation camp. Life had come full circle: my father's journey to the Far East had started out in these barracks, home of the KNIL unit where he received his first army training before setting sail in 1936.

The barracks were made of wood with tin roofs and offered the most basic of accommodation. Being a larger family, with four children, two rooms were allocated, a living space and a bedroom, with just jute sacks filled with straw for beds which had to be turned and stamped flat regularly – a task the boys enjoyed thoroughly. All six of us had to share this one bedroom so there was no privacy at all. The whole 'camp' was fenced off with chicken mesh, and the camp owner lived in a house by the gate. In truth, it was in many ways an echo of the conditions in the prison camps my parents and brothers had endured all those years.

The camp was home to the European Dutch repatriates as well as the mixed-race Dutch Indonesians, called *Indos'*, who were housed separately within the complex, resulting in tensions between the different groups. To make matters worse, crowds of local Dutch used to gather daily at the fence, shouting abuse, calling us '*uitzuigers*' (leeches, suckers), and *Indos*, echoing the general feeling among the Dutch about all returnees from the colony. One day Jantje got so mad at one boy who was shouting abuse at him that he climbed over the fence, ran after him and gave him a good hiding right near his house. When the boy's father came out and asked why he was beating up his son, Jantje said that his son was always calling him an *Indo* and that he was fed up with it because he was Dutch, just like him and his son.

There was a strong feeling in Holland that the country had suffered so much during Nazi occupation and had ended up so totally impoverished, that they did not want all those colonial repatriates who had come back penniless and were now expecting to be fed and housed. To help ease the housing shortage following this influx the Dutch government had made – often financially attractive – arrangements with many owners of large houses to create the so-called 'contract pensions' (a sort of guesthouse). Some of these pensions were very good and well run; others had miserable owners who provided below-standard accommodation, but usually there was just one room per family.

After about a year and a half in the barracks we moved to such a pension in a small village called Ederveen. It was an old Dutch-style castle called *Bruinhorst*, which in its heyday would have been an amazing place, and still exists today. Nearby was a farm where we used to play with the animals – 'horse riding' on the cows for example, sitting backwards using the tail as a kind of rein. Olaf taught us girls how to catch fish in the big pond in front of the castle: with a tin stuck on the end of a long stick, to scoop up the fish in a very deft way.

Our fun at the farm in Ederveen did not last very long, and

we soon moved to a pension in the nearby town of Lunteren, called *De Boekhorst,* much more spacious and set in beautiful grounds that were filled with the most colourful rhododendron bushes. At the front there was a lovely balcony from where we all stood to watch the annual arrival in December of *Sinterklaas* (St Nicholas, the Dutch Father Christmas), a tradition growing ever more popular as the years go by.

For Jan and Olaf life soon started to return to some normality as they now had to go to school. Jan remembers walking past a house each day where a nice dog sat outside, and of course the boys would make a fuss over the dog. An English lady lived there and one day around Christmas time she invited the boys in for a cup of tea and gave them a little Christmas tree decoration: an angel that according to English tradition would sit on the top of the tree. This little angel topped our Christmas trees for years to come.

Having consistently ignored my father's requests for proper housing for the family, the Army authorities were about to transfer my father yet again to some other part of the country. My mother, who knew that the constant refusals were in part due to her nationality, eventually became so outraged that she went to the Army housing department and demanded her family be moved out of the contract pension and into a home suitable for a family of six.

Finally, towards the end of 1953, we were allocated a house of our own in the army town of Ede. Life now could return to some sort of normality, and for a while it was good. We got Slamper the dog, a cat, a stray bird and a rabbit in the garden, which was sadly eaten one Christmas. But, as so often happens in families torn apart by war, relationships suffer too much to ever really be cemented back together again, and this was no different for our parents. Their ordeals in the camps and their sheer determination to ensure their survival, especially for my mother who had to take care of the boys, had changed them both. Just like most survivors, neither of them spoke much about their experiences. My brother Jan remembers that in the beginning he and Olaf often asked questions about the camp, wanting to learn more about that time and why it all happened, but that they were told it was history and they should just forget it. When they both completed school they became sailors and left home, Our parents stayed together for the sake of us girls but they were clearly desperately unhappy and just made each other's life a misery. Sadly, they could not overcome their differences and in 1965 their marriage ended.

Acknowledgements

My very special thanks go to Roberte Swain-Halberstadt, translator of the original Dutch version of *The House at Ampasiet*. Rob (as she prefers to be called) was actually born in such a camp, namely Camp Karees in Bandoeng and I met her via the BBC WW2 website. We spent hours talking about camp experiences and I learned so much from her about those years. Rob devoted an amazing amount of time and energy to verify sources and check historical accuracy for the Dutch version, and while working with me on that she simultaneously produced a first English sight-translation of the book. She was a special inspiration; without her drive and enthusiasm this English version would not have seen the light of day.

I have also been lucky to have a great editorial team to help get this version into shape, and wholeheartedly thank each of them: Fran Howarth who tackled the first major edit, and as a native English speaker gave great suggestions for improvements; Peta Eisberg, the major editor of the original Dutch version who proved as sharp as ever in her work on grammar and punctuation of this English version. Having spent so much time on the Dutch version, she could ensure any edits were all in line with my mother's original meanings and intentions; Katherine Ross, herself a professional writer, who made invaluable comments on style and layout, and provided that final and most important editorial 'sanity check'. Finally Carolyn Fuller, my professional proof reader who also provided essential support with the photographic material.

I am hugely indebted to Dr. Bernice Archer, for her tremendous help and suggestions on the additional chapter, and for agreeing to write a Foreword. As a historian, Bernice wrote at length about the internment of women in Japanese prison camps in her thesis *The Internment of Western Civilians under the Japanese 1941/1945*, now published in hardback as *The Internment of Western Civilians under the Japanese 1941-1945: A Patchwork of Internment (London: RoutledgeCurzon, 2004)*, and in paperback under the same title by Hong Kong University Press, 2008.

I also wish to thank Pieter Tesch, like me a post-war child of Dutch parentage, who has made the post-war period of Indonesia's struggle for independence his special focus and was able to give very valuable background information to help me make sense of my father's notes.

Ton Hardeman, a young artist in The Netherlands, who originally worked with my mother to create the cover design for the Dutch version of the book, deserves a special mention. For this English version his original design was again the basis for the front cover, while Ton also created some additional drawings in a similar style.

I also thank each and everyone here in England, who listened so patiently to my endless talking about this great book that one day would have to be published in English, no matter what, to make sure my mother's story would reach as wide an audience as possible.

Bibliography and photography

Due to the fact that this is a posthumous publication, there was no opportunity for me to verify certain anecdotes or claims and comments for historical accuracy with my parents. Especially for the additional chapters *Jan's Story* and *Rebuilding Life*, much needed to be gleaned from notes left behind and from, now vague, family recollections. I therefore spent a lot of time researching historical data, not only of those years of captivity, but also of Europe prior to the Second World War. I also read some of the accounts published by other survivors to get my mind into the period and the mood of the time. I recognised how the survivors recounted identical experiences, yet always from their own individual and often unique perspective, each story needing to be told. I would like to thank all those whose stories are out there for having told them for all of us to share and remember. I hope *The House at Ampasiet* will contribute to that wealth in its own way.

The great majority of photographic material is from our own family albums and resources. Where I managed to locate the sources of specific additional photo material, written permission has been granted, and appropriate credits and source references have been given in each picture caption. There were however a few pictures whose sources I was unable to verify. Anyone who has identified any material not referenced should contact me via the publisher for post production clearance. Also, despite all my research and the intensive editing efforts, there may of course be other inaccuracies and errors. I would welcome feedback, which can be forwarded to the publisher in the first instance.

The following books have been specifically mentioned in the text and where material has been accessed for reference purposes, contact was made with the publishers and permission granted.

Archer, Bernice (2004/2008) – *The Internment of Western Civilians under the Japanese 1941-1945, A Patchwork of Internment* – London: RoutledgeCurzon, 2004, and paperback under the same title by Hong Kong University Press, 2008.

Hamel, J.C. (1948) – *Soldatendominee* – N.V. Uitgeverij W. van Hoeve, 's Gravenhage, Netherlands.

Hillen, Ernest (1944) *The Way of a Boy: A Memoir of Java* – Viking (Canada and Britain)

McGeoch Angus (2002) – *Hitler's Children* (from the original German: Knopp, Guido (2000) – (Hitler's Kinder) – Sutton Publishing Limited, UK.

Velden, Dr D. van (1985, 4e druk) – *De Japanse Interneringskampen voor Burgers Gedurende de Tweede Wereldoorlog (The Japanese Civil Internment Camps During the Second World War)* – Uitgeverij T. Wever B.V., Franeker, Netherlands.